The Gift Inside the Wound

A Divorce Memoir

Teri Leigh

MOZI Publications

Copyright © 2017 by Teri Leigh
All rights reserved.

Cover Artwork by Amanda Meyer
www.amandammeyer.com

All right reserved. No part of this book may be reproduced or transmitted in any form or by any means, electronic or mechanical, including photocopying, recording, or by any information storage and retrieval system, without permission in writing directly from TeriLeigh.

The scanning, uploading, and distribution of any content in this book via the internet or via any other means without the permission of the publisher is illegal and punishable by law. Please purchase only authorized electronic editions, and do no participate in or encourage electronic piracy of copyrighted materials. Your support of the author's rights is appreciated.

Printed in the United State of America

ISBN-13 paperback: 978-0-9859643-7-5
ISBN-13 ebook: 978-0-9859643-8-2

More by Teri Leigh

BOOKS

30 Days of Muchness: A Mindfulness Program for Eating, Exercise, and Meditation

The Gift Inside the Wound

MOZI Your Way to Mindfulness

The Shadow's Shine: The Summer of 1985

Yoga Wonderland: Adventures in Home Practice

ONLINE LEARNING PROGRAMS

Body Wisdom: Mindfulness in Healthy Posture & Mechanics

The Goldilocks Principle: A Practical Guide to the Chakras

The MOZI Method for Mindfulness

Yoga Wonderland: Adventures in Home Practice

www.MindfulnessOnlineAcademy.com
www.TeriLeigh.com

Praise for The Gift Inside the Wound

"This memoir is like listening to a close friend pour out her heart over a bottle of wine."

"This story is raw, deep and intense and causes you to reflect on your own wounds and your own journey in healing. I had trouble putting this book down and found myself laughing out loud, to tears welling in my eyes."

"I had to make myself put The Gift Inside the Wound down so I would be able to 'spend more time' with TeriLeigh. Truthfully the whole book captivated me. It was like I was riding along in the car with her, in the back seat as each personified emotion sat in the front with her. I could feel the coldness of the air, and the sting of grief and sorrow every time she mentioned them."

"Teri Leigh, through this book and through her very being, has helped validate my own grief process. I felt her presence on each and every page, as though she were there speaking right to me."

"This is a raw, emotional book that reminds you there is a light at the end of difficult times. If you enjoyed reading "Eat, Pray, Love" this is similar, but with more descriptive emotions that makes you feel like you are experiencing this along with Teri Leigh."

*For every woman
who was broken
and healed herself
from the inside out.*

Preface

*"There are things known and things unknown.
In between are the doors of perception."*
~Aldous Huxley

Healing is the transition space, the doorway portal between the known and the unknown. The unknown is both a scary and exciting place. When we suffer a wound of trauma or tragedy, we are forced into the unknown, a free fall without knowing when or where or how we might land.

In the plane, I am safe. Locked inside the pressurized cabin, I am a ticketed passenger gazing out my tiny portal windows at the silver airplane wing. Inside the plane, the world of the plane cabin seems very real and tangible. As they roll metal carts smiling attendants bring you bottled drinks and cracker snacks wrapped in cellophane wrappers. I can adjust the airflow of my own personal fan by turning a nozzle just so. Inside the cabin, I can drift through the sky without a thought or a care in the world.

We don't want to leave the land we call Familiar. We love its yellow painted comfort zone guidelines. With clearly written expectations, and known variables we feel a false sense of security, as if everything can and should go as visualized, and planned. But, the land of structure and organization is limiting... boring even.

The wilderness of clouds are on the other side of the portal window. "DO NOT WALK OUTSIDE THIS AREA" is printed in bold black block letters across the wing. This stern warning reminds me of the laws and rules that must be followed so that I stay safely confined within the tightly packed rows of seats, storage bins, and safety belts. Securing my seatbelt across my lap in the center seat wedged between indecision and discomfort certainly wasn't comfortable anymore, but it was familiar.

At the same time, there is a sense of adventure in all of us. A yearning to walk out of this area, to break the rules. A desire to taste the grass on the other side of the fence, to know the world on the other side of the wall. What is fearful and anxiety driven on the right foot is exciting and thrilling on the left.

The silver airplane wing hangs out there, floating and still. The wings of birds are graceful and feather-light and flexible. But this fixed unbendable metal wing seems more mechanical than anything made of nature. Set against the pale organic blue backdrop of pure air, the silver wing gleams in the cloudless light. I longed to get out of my seat, to crawl out of my tiny portal window and stand out there on the area where the rules say we are not supposed to be.

The unknown is the greatest of all fears. Think about it—the three most common fears are death, public speaking, and heights. All of these have the unknown in common. Many of us choose being uncomfortable in the familiar over facing the unknown. Yet, facing the unknown is a human condition that no one can escape.

Even if we are stuck in the rut of indecision, we cannot stay frozen forever because life continues to move around us. When we stand frozen at the crossroads of indecision and confusion, something outside of our control happens. Inevitably, we run out of sky. Something pushes us from behind, or swipes us from the side, or sweeps us off our feet and forces us over the rumble strip of our comfort zone into the big bad unknown.

More often than not, that push or swipe or sweep appears in the form of a trauma, leaving a bloody wound in its wake. Ready or not, we jump, usually beaten and broken from our own resistance, into a place where the roads aren't mapped out and our GPS has no signal, groping our way through the dark.

Fuck You Sunday forced me to step out of the comfort of the pressurized cabin of traditional marriage, and walk into what I thought was the forbidden realm of potential divorce. I found myself surfing on the wing of the plane, the words "DO NOT WALK OUTSIDE THIS AREA" underneath my toes and absolutely nothing to grip onto. I looked over the edge and peered into the unknown vastness of natural water blue sky. Part of me gazed off into the distance with curiosity and anticipation at the vast possibilities of what I could never know. I relished the idea of riding the current.

And so, I let myself be pushed from behind, swept off my feet.
I let go.

In the portal between the discomfort of familiar and the thrill of the unknown, feeling for light switches, we may catch our fingers on exposed rusty nails and stub our toes on knotty roots. The demons of the mind play a constant game of cat and mouse with our emotions. We are challenged by Grief and Loneliness, Fear and Anxiety, Guilt and Regret. We stumble upon other wounds, invisible wounds, buried within memories, deep inside brain cells.

In the initial free fall I was tossed in the wind, whisked into a hurricane, and drenched by sleet. I lost all my senses, except one. Blinded by the darkness, deafened by the silence, my sense of feeling heightened. My wounds were too deep and too raw to be erased or washed clean by the outside rain and fog. My healing had to happen from the inside out. In order to fully heal I had to FEEL, because the only way out is through. Through the unknown.

Different from the physical wounds that bleed or leave a visible scar, easy to identify and treat, invisible wounds are far out of reach of physical therapy or the setting of a broken bone or the stitching and bandaging of a deep laceration. For invisible wounds, healing is not solved with medication or surgery; rather, it comes while we grope around in the dark unknown edges of our lives, searching for a light.

Light switches come to in the form of friends, mentors, insights, and experiences.

Once I surrendered to my falling fate, then and only then was I able to recognize the dozens of angels soaring on fully expanded wings forming a safety net all around me. They came in many costumes wearing techni-color wings—a breast cancer survivor, a Vietnam vet and his therapy dog, a transgender man, a dominatrix, and many more—empowered me with healing salves of inner strength and confidence and love. Most importantly, they showed me how to see past the storm into the sunshine hidden behind it; they taught me how to cross a minus to make a plus, and flip a negative to a positive.

Healing isn't always comfortable. Yes, it can be beautiful and loving and tender. And it can be ugly and painful. Whatever we are healing from, we can encounter numerous lights and illuminations. And the spaces between those lights can be dark and dreary. In the search for healing the gashes of our wounds, we journey into the unknown spaces in our souls. That journey, the space between known and unknown, we ultimately drink the marrow of life and discover our greatest gifts.

These angels welcomed me to their dinner tables and guest bedrooms across America…Minnesota to South Dakota, Iowa to Florida, Vermont to Hawaii, and New York to Ohio. From a New Year's grief ritual at a northern Minnesota cabin in the dead of winter to a cleansing Easter rebirth in a sacred bay of Maui, I offered my tears to Old Man Winter, bowed to Mother Earth, and prayed to the Hawaiian Goddess Pele.

When I landed on my own two feet, I realized that I was never really comfortable in the blissful ignorance of stowed luggage and seat tray tables that hide neatly away. I refused to stuff several "fuck you's" into the overhead compartment, because going to sleep and waking up at a destination of yesterday was pointless and painful. Besides, the cabin door of my past had been shut and latched.

The Healing Process

THE WOUND — 4
- The Wounding ~ Facing the Unknown — 5
  - Fuck You Sunday — 6

THE HEALING — 14
- First Aid ~ Feeling Safe — 15
  - A Security Blanket — 16
  - Flooded With Compliments — 22
- Cleaning the Wound ~ Letting Go — 28
  - Grief's Grip On My Throat — 30
  - Sweating Out the Tears — 38
  - Making Friends with Grief — 46
- Stitching the Wound ~ Feeling Strong — 52
  - Whatever Makes You Happy. Do That. — 54
  - Empowerment of the Red Queen — 64
  - The Panther's Desire — 72
- Bandaging the Wound ~ Receiving Love — 80
  - Yes, Thank You — 82
  - The Labrador Lean — 88
  - Now-ness and Power-Posing — 92

THE GIFT — 98
- Time to Heal ~ Turning Within — 99
  - Solitude and a Long Stretch of Alone Time — 100
  - Love is a State of Being — 106
- Removing the Bandages ~ Moving Forward — 115
  - A Different Point of View — 116
  - Surrender and Let Go — 120
  - Look Up and Have Faith — 128
  - A Soul Cleansing — 134
- Loving the Scars ~ Celebrating Success — 141
  - Rainbow Eucalyptus Scars — 142
  - Objects in Mirror Are Closer Than They Appear — 148
  - Bless Me, Saturday — 154

Blessing	158
THE TEACHING	**160**
Finding the Gifts Inside Your Own Wounds	161
A Letter to My Readers	162

Itinerary

JANUARY
Backus MN
Sioux Falls SD

FEBRUARY
Clermont FL
Apollo Beach FL
Tampa FL

MARCH
Wilmington NC
Asheville NC
Washington DC
Towson MD
Manchester VT

APRIL
Maui HI
New York City, NY
Westerly RI
Gloucester MA
Natick MA

MAY
Yorkville IL
Brookfield WI
Sussex WI
Minneapolis MN

JUNE
Cleveland OH

The wound is the place where the light enters you.
~Rumi

What you are about to read is my life's greatest wound.

The Sunday after Christmas 2012, a day I now refer to as "Fuck You Sunday," my husband asked for a divorce so he could live the life of a celibate monk. Looking back, the scene seems like a contradiction—my scholarly, yogic-scripture-quoting, and meditation driven husband pushed me over a dining room chair while screaming "fuck you" in rage, shattering every emotional bone of my being.

And so, I fell into the abysmal space of the unknown.

THE WOUND

The Wounding ~ Facing the Unknown

Fuck You Sunday

"Be sure to taste your words before you spit them out."
~Auliq Ice

I don't know if it matters that it happened on a Sunday or that it happened after Christmas 2012. But it happened. I was on the floor, looking up at the ceiling of my house and at my husband's angry face glaring down on me. He had pushed me down, over the dining room chair, and was looming over me, red-faced and angry, daggers in his eyes. A school teacher, a supposedly spiritual man who practiced daily meditation, spat out the two words intending to pierce my eardrums, break my heart, splinter my soul.

F u c k   Y o u

He stabbed me repeatedly with those two huge little words and told me he wanted a divorce so he could live the life of a celibate monk. Rather a contradiction, my husband cussing at me so he could be a monk. Aren't monks meant to be peaceful? Evidently, his hours of meditation and scriptural study didn't make him immune to the human emotions of rage.

His verbal assault felt worse than the date rape I endured in college. I was left with a massive wound, a giant gash in my earth. While he didn't use the c-word at me that day, and he didn't physically rape me, his words felt like the deepest violation I had ever endured in my thirty-nine years on the planet. When it was all done, my entire world shifted. An earthquake, and I was left gripping the edge while he stepped on my fingers.

Saying 'Fuck You' once is nothing. Most of us say it in traffic once a week. We hear it on HBO or Netflix several times an episode. We're used to it. We say it to our friends and loved ones like a term of endearment or a special privilege. With the right smile and an inside joke, intimate friends who trust each other tell each other to lovingly fuck off.

But when we mean it, that's when it hurts. Like the rubber balloon you've been squeezing suddenly pops, that's when 'Fuck You' is weaponized, and becomes a sharp object that does what it was meant to do—to stab and violate and hurt.

I did not know it at the time, but when Ted pounded my eardrums with the two words I hated the most in the world, the doors of the airplane cabin burst open, and I was ripped out of my safe seat and hurled into the wide vast blue unknown, away from everything I knew.

While I'd heard those words escape Ted's lips many times in our eleven years as a couple, he never pointed them directly at me. On the other hand, I was no stranger to feeling those words aimed in my direction. As a high school teacher of at-risk youth, I had learned to shield myself from impact, and deflect their energy. Vulgarity has never really hurt me before. But that day, those two words repeated like a mantra, burned me like a red-hot brand directly on the rawness of my heart.

The ubiquitous word speaks volumes, not by its definitions or connotations, but by its energy. It carries with it an invisible and mutable arrow, capable of making any discourse turn from drab to techni-color. It can make all ears within range buzz from its unique frequency. The combination of sounds in the word, the soft F and the sharp —ck blend to energetically re-tune the frequency of anything it attaches to or strikes. While short and sharp, the sound resonates like the ripple of a boulder dropped into a still pond, disturbing and adjusting everything around it, underneath it, inside it, and even above it.

My family respected the potency of the F-word while Ted's family instinctively diminished its power through overuse. To my family, the vulgarity was as foreign to our tongues as rolling r's are to non-Latin speakers. Ted's dad used it often, to describe anything and everything distasteful, as well as to emphasize joy or excitement. As a result, Ted could change the meaning of words, while I was confined to dictionary definitions.

Ted and I are both English teachers by training, educated to value and respect the structure and culture of language, burdened with the responsibility to teach the youth of Midwestern America to effectively communicate. Yet, our own means of expression are diametrically opposed. Ted speaks in a language that can numb and desensitize, while I speak a language of emotion meant to heighten and ignite. He takes big bites of words and swallows whole while I cut syllables into tiny pieces and suck the flavor, ingesting the essence on my tongue before swallowing it to my core. One day we eventually found ourselves 10 years into marriage without the ability to communicate.

"I'm trying to figure out a way out," he said blankly. His face froze in a cold stare. I swallowed his sentence whole, feeling the thorn of the word "out" scratching the interior walls of my esophagus. When it reached my stomach, I felt all air sucked from my lungs.

He had said the unimaginable. I grew up in a family where divorce just didn't happen. It was inconceivable. My parents, and my grandparents, and all my aunts and uncles were still together, until death do they part. With one little sentence and an icy cold stare, he pushed me outside of my comfort zone, forced me to step away from the familiar, and shoved me into the world of who-knows-what-happens-next.

I knew that anything I said might just bounce right off of him, my own emotions ricocheting back at me.

"If that's what you want, then just do it. Get out." I stood up and pointed to the door. We'd had the conversation many times, about how I thought he was disrespecting me by not pulling his weight around the house, by not contributing to the relationship, not communicating with me about his life. For the last three years I had felt more like his housemaid and roommate than his wife.

"I'm trying to figure out how," he said quietly.

"GET OUT NOW! If you wanna be a monk and live a solitary life devoted to meditation and scriptural study, stop pretending and just go do it. You've had plenty of time to figure it out. You've had three years of treating me like this. Your time is up."

"You can't just kick me out. I live here too. I pay most of the mortgage."

"Get Out." Those two words were all I had left.

"Fuck you! You always have to have things your way. You want what you want!" His voice began to elevate, and for a moment emotion took him over.

There it hit. For just a moment, he spoke in my language of emotion.

"GET OUT."

"FUCK YOU."

"GET OUT."

"FUCK YOU."

"GET OUT."

"FUCK YOU."

"GET OUT."

"I FUCKING HATE YOU." He pushed me over a chair onto the floor. He glared down at me, rage written all over his face, daggers spitting from his eyes. Giant icicles penetrated deep beneath my rib cage, deflated my lungs and punctured my heart over and over again, leaving a chill that froze me from the marrow of my bones outward.

Who was this man with coldness that bites worse than wind chill in Minnesota winters? This man I married, who treated that word before as insignificant as the leftover dust in a cereal bag was now using it to its full potency, against me, the wife he had vowed to love for the rest of our lives. I defended myself with the only protection I knew, the same two words I had used with high school students when they used the f-word on me.

"Get out." It came out as a whisper.

"You can't make me," Ted responded exactly the same way as my students had, mocking my small physical stature and testing my will. Yet, I had filled a toolbox of skills for situations like this after years of dealing with juvenile delinquents. My tools hadn't ever failed me with them, and they worked again with Ted. I got up from the floor. Maneuvered the chair upright between us, planted my feet on the ground and said it again.

"Get out." The words came from my core. I felt my belly heat up with internal fire, resolve, conviction. Entirely different from the rage he showed me only a moment ago.

"I live here too," his voice quivered.

"You said 'fuck you' repeatedly and pushed me over a chair onto the floor. I can call the police and have you physically removed for domestic abuse." I replaced the hammer of "get out" with the hatchet, knowing that if I had to, I could add some barbs by picking up the phone.

Just like the kids at school, Ted was taken aback, half in disbelief that I could even say such a thing, and half in sheer terror that I would follow through. At first, his ire was raised, and he took a step towards me as if to strike. But, I stood my ground, using the coldness that he had injected into me with his fuck-you icicles against him, and he surrendered.

"I don't hate you. I didn't mean that. Can't we discuss this like adults?"

"Just go." The words escaped as a whisper this time. I stood up and retreated to my sanctuary in the basement while he packed his stuff. That day was not the first time I had accused him of being a monk and he had accused me of being needy. But, that day was the first time he used the f-word against me. Our relationship was devolving into the realm of abusive. I curled up in the fetal position in front of my meditation altar with pictures of my ancestors gazing lovingly at me as if to say, "Stay strong, let him go."

Ted is good at letting go. One of his favorite pictures is of the Indian guru, Nityananda, whose hands were perfect expressions of non-attachment, his hands open, fingers spread evenly, completely devoid of wrinkles and stress from any grip. The only thing Ted gripped with any intensity was his discipline towards his spiritual practice, the perfect oxymoron. A renunciate, he valued wide-open space and felt smothered by clutter. Junk drawers and overstuffed closets were as toxic to him as ammonia is to bleach. Ultimately renunciation meant letting go of all attachments, evidently that included the vows he had made to me.

I'm no stranger to letting go either, but until "Fuck You Sunday" I employed the practice of letting go of one thing only so that I may grasp onto something else, preferably of better quality. I sold my house, quit my job, and moved my world to marry him, the man my mother picked out for me, because that is what the woman does, and it was an upgrade from single life in a smaller town. I pictured our marriage like our two hands folded together, fingers interwoven in a way that we couldn't tell mine from his, the exact opposite of Nityananda's. My marriage was the greatest treasure I had ever grasped, and I couldn't imagine trading it in for anything else in the world. But this time, I had no choice. He had let go, and I couldn't hold on anymore.

While meditation had always been a priority in his life that I had supported, when the morning alarm started going off at 4 a.m. and earlier so he could meditate when the rest of the world was still, I resisted. When he would get out of bed, and his energy left my space, I felt as though the comforter had been pulled off of me. While 5 a.m. could work with my sleep cycle, that meant Ted would lay in bed staring at the ceiling, antsy and uncomfortable for 45 minutes to an hour until I was ready to wake. When he suggested separate bedrooms, I felt one of his fingers loosen its grip away from mine. Eventually, I let go of sleeping late in trade for my own early morning routine of yoga and meditation and a daily walk with our dog.

The more we fought about wake-up times and he argued for separate bedrooms, the less he wanted sex. To him, ejaculation was an extreme expenditure of spiritual energy that worked in direct conflict with his spiritual practice. To me, sex was the ultimate union of the masculine and feminine energies, the merging of the yin and yang. When he experimented with tantric exercises to withhold ejaculation, I felt another finger of his release its grip from my hand. When his sexual drive diminished and he leaned towards celibacy, a third finger released from my hand. I had a choice, give up sex or give up my husband. I loved him, and I wanted him to be happy, so I tightened my grip on his hand with only two fingers left and released sexuality in trade for creative expression. I started writing more, travelling more, and teaching more. I built a small name for myself as a travelling yoga instructor and spiritual teacher.

While Ted retreated further and further into his hermit cave of meditation and celibacy, my career flourished, and I developed a large network of friends and clients across the country. I'd go away for a week or two making connections with people all over America while he'd retreat deep into his cave, coming out only for teaching school, and daily ten minute telephone conversations with me and his mother. I joked with my friends that Ted's level of being social was equal to my own level of being anti-social. Over several months, I started to recognize that he didn't want to go on any social outings when I was home. He'd long since let all his own friendships evaporate, and was pulling away from our mutual friends as well. While I distracted myself by booking jobs that took me further away for longer and developing deeper connections with my friends on the road, he had let go of one more finger, leaving me to hold the marriage together by gripping his palm and his one pinky finger.

Fuck You Sunday, Ted pulled his hand away from me entirely. When I refused to reach to catch it again, I noticed that his hands looked just like Nityananda's in the photo, empty, flat, completely free of grip.

Teri Leigh

THE HEALING

Teri Leigh

First Aid ~ Feeling Safe

The Gift Inside the Wound

A Security Blanket

> *"A mother's arms are made of tenderness*
> *and children sleep soundly in them."*
> *~Victor Hugo*

After Ted left the house, I went into shock. I don't know if I actually passed out, but I certainly did lose time. Cowered under the cover of my meditation shawl in front of my ancestor shrine, sounds dulled with the density in my head. But, the smell of my own breath under the shawl seemed more pungent than ever before. While my head was heavy, my body felt light, and with just a few breaths, I felt like I'd been sucked up into a tornado time warp. I felt myself shrink from the size of a full-grown woman into my toddler self. Visions and sensations of my childhood flooded my senses. I landed in memories where mommy's kiss and a boo-boo-bunny could make every owie better. My meditation shawl shape-shifted into my childhood Blankie, my blanket of security.

Blankie was my best friend. On good days, she carried my found treasures wrapped up like a present. On bad days, I buried my face in her folds, and she'd absorb my tears. I soothed all my fear and anxiety by squeezing her corner in my fist while sucking my thumb.

Then one day, she was gone.

When the lid closed on the washer I sat on the concrete floor of the dingy basement laundry room and waited for her to come back from the Unknown. As she had been there for me through the worst, I couldn't leave her when she went into somewhere potentially unsafe. The water might drown her!

In her rumpled crevices, she had gathered all the emotions of every experience I ever had in those three years. I didn't want those dissolved in water and Tide detergent. When Mom reached into the washer tub, Blankie came out in clumped matted pieces, wet dreadlocks. I felt like my own hair had been ripped out from my scalp. Those matted clumps of Blankie might as well have been my intestines because I felt like my insides had been shredded. I broke into uncontrollable blubbering sobs, temper tantrum wails, my hands pulling at my hair, my legs flailing.

My mother, always the first responder, made herself into a blanket and wrapped around me. I buried my face in her chest until I exhausted myself and fell asleep. I awoke sometime later, still wrapped in the arms of my mother, cozy on the family room couch. Remembering that Blankie was gone, I sighed. I was a big girl now.

Ted's hand in my own was as soothing to me as an adult as Blankie's corner in my thumb sucking fist was to me as a toddler. The shrieking crash of his "Fuck You" was worse than the sound of the washing machine lid slamming down. I had to be a grown up now. No more husband to smooth the wrinkles out of my life.

But I wasn't ready to grow up…Not just yet.

Curled in the fetal position under the security blanket of my meditation shawl, my grown-up toddler self wanted my Mommy. I couldn't tell if it was instinct or old childhood patterns that led me to dial the phone. I suspect that my grandmother Florence reached her wrinkled and weathered hand out of her portrait on my ancestor shrine and moved my fingers on the keypad. I called Mommy, my emotional 9-1-1.

I looked up from under my meditation cloth at the shrine of ancestor photos I had built. For years I sat in front of these pictures in meditation, praying to these souls whose collective DNA brought me to this planet. My grandmother Florence and my great aunt, Virginia, my two most recently deceased family members from my mother's side, held significant spots in the shrine. Their portraits stood on my great aunt's white crocheted shawl, a vestige she wore once upon a time, perhaps for her own emotional sense of security. Their two pictures each had an old-fashioned watch they had worn draped over the corner of their picture frame. The red-headed sisters represented the strength of the feminine line in my blood, always taking their seats together as hostesses sharing the head of the dining room table of every family gathering.

They gazed lovingly down at me as I shivered under my security meditation shawl, waiting for Mommy. I had never seen either of them cry. Neither of them ever expressed disappointment or frustration towards me. That day, I thought that maybe they would frown at me in pity.

They didn't.

Instead, they smiled with pride, as they always did, making the biggest deal out of even my smallest accomplishments. I don't know if they were proud that I had kicked Ted out or that I had called my mother. It didn't matter. Try as I might, I couldn't reject their pride. So I let myself once again get sucked back into the tornado of emotions. I fell back into shock, and surrendered to memories of childhood.

Whenever I was scared, Grandma was always there. When I was five years old, Grandma watched from her front step as I walked alone to kindergarten on my second day of school. When I played a piano solo in front of the whole school in a competition, Grandma stood up in the audience to give me someone to focus on instead of the hugeness of the crowd. At 16, when I drove to her house by myself to show her my new driver's license, I pulled out of her driveway in front of a cop while Grandma stood on her front step, smiling and waving. To this day, I swear that her loving wave must have softened the cop's heart enough to not pull me over and give me a ticket. Years later, while backpacking through Europe in college, I learned my grandfather died unexpectedly. Grandma's stern voice through the pay phone told me to stay in Brussels and enjoy a glass of wine in the Grand Place and salute the Mannekin de Pis (a tiny statue of a boy peeing) instead of flying home for the funeral.

I was 35 when I said goodbye to Grandma on Christmas Eve. On her death bed, she told me she'd never leave me. I believed her because she had always been there for me during the most scared and thus the most sacred times of my life. I had no doubt that she could continue to do so without the benefit of a human body. She died Christmas morning.

In my tornado shock of memories, Grandma Florence and her sister Virginia came back to life. They wrapped me in their arms and held me close for over an hour until my mother arrived.

Mom found me on the floor in front of my shrine. Like she did in the laundry room 36 years earlier, she wrapped me in the blanket of herself. Her firm embrace was deep pressure on my wounds, enough to stop the bleeding and treat my shock.

While time had wrinkled her face and softened her belly, everything else about that moment felt exactly as it had when I was three. The soft pillow of her breasts under my cheek felt vaguely of the vibrations of lullabies from her lips. Her soft kiss on the top of my head, her nose inhaling the scent of my hair sent a cascade of warm soothing waves down my spinal cord. Nestling into her womb was the only thing in the world that could make me feel safe and secure again. I sobbed into her breasts. She allowed her blouse to become drenched with my tears.

She made it safe for me to cry.
She made it okay for me to let go.

My tornado stopped spinning. My senses returned, and I could once again hear the ticking of time. I didn't exactly feel entirely okay, but I was more okay than before she had arrived. Her touch and her voice made me realized I wasn't going to die. This wasn't the end. I could breathe again.

Mom's heart was strong, having withheld the sobs and pains of three children for over 40 years. It had been many years since I had physically laid my face on my mother's breast, but in that moment as my head lifted and lowered to the rhythm of my mother's breath, I knew she would always see me and hold me and love me as the newborn infant who suckled nourishment from her nipples. Every inhale served to suck the pain from my sobs into her lungs and heart. Between each breath was this tiny moment of stillness, a place where the external world seemed to stop momentarily so that my pain could alchemize inside my mother's heart. Through the compression of her heart muscles, the dense and dull lead-heavy ache was washed and pressurized with the full redness of her blood and turned to a viscous gold-light fluid that pressed into me with every exhale. The remnants of my pain she couldn't transform washed down the walls of her insides from her heart into her belly, like water crying from the crevices of a mountain ridge seeking their source in the pools and rivers below.

My mother greeted the ugliness of Grief in a way I didn't know how. She welcomed Him into her arms with gratitude and embraced him like an old friend. She had communed with him five years earlier when she was diagnosed with uterine cancer just weeks after Grandma died. Within a month, she grieved the loss of her mother and her uterus, her childhood and her womanhood.

Shortly after a hysterectomy, dopey from the pain medicine and anesthetic, she looked at me with clear eyes and said, "Teri, you're never really grown up until both your parents are dead."

I didn't know what to say. Her words were so powerful, like Truth had bubbled up right out of her mouth and spilled all over me, leaving a sticky film I couldn't wash off.

She blessed me with age-old wisdom. At the same time, she sternly instructed me that it was time to grow up.

Being the middle child, the only daughter, I was the one who had stayed close to my parents while both my brothers had moved out of state long ago. I was the kid who attended all the family gatherings, met my parents for dinner for every holiday, called them to help with odd jobs around my house, and traded dog-sitting duties. I was the kid who was in contact with my parents almost every day while my brothers could sometimes go months without a word. All my life I thought that made me the responsible one, but that day in the hospital room I recognized that it also meant I was the one who had probably grown up the least.

I went running to Mommy many times as a not-quite-grown-up-grown-up.

After graduating college, I suffered depression and played chicken with the on-coming semi trucks of Wisconsin farm roads more than once. Mom came to live with me, cook my favorite meals, and take me to a psychiatrist. She coached me through trading Zoloft for cardio-kickboxing and weight training. Years later, when I suffered severe complications from asthma and bronchitis induced by a deadly allergy to cats, Mom researched and found and paid for an expensive alternative treatment so that I could one day board an airplane without fear of sitting next to someone with deadly cat dander on their clothing. At 27, I moved back in with Mom and Dad for eight months between jobs. At 35, I asked them to bail me out of a bad business partnership, and they loaned me a lot of money, knowing full well I would probably never be able to pay them back.

I never REALLY grew up.

At 39 years old, while crying in my mother's arms after Ted left, I made a very conscious decision. I didn't want to wait until both she and Dad were dead to really grow up. I decided it was time to find a way to rid myself of the sticky film of my mother's hospital prophecy from under my skin. It was time to close the washing machine lid on the emotional security blankets I had sewn into the fabric of my life.

It was time to put on my grown-up pants.

When she hugged me goodbye that day, she invited me to come home with them until I got back on my feet. I told her that I wanted to do this on my own.

Flooded With Compliments

"A compliment is verbal sunshine."
~Robert Orben

In the days that followed the storm of Fuck You Sunday, several more first responders offered me first-aid healing. Staying at the house where I lived with Ted felt like staying at the scene of the crime. Since I'd made the decision to grow up, I refused to go back home with my parents. Instead, I visited with various friends and family in the Twin Cities, bouncing around from dinner table to guest bed like a ping pong ball. I'd meet one friend for lunch, another for dinner, and crash at someone else's place at night. Each one of them received me with a gentle affection, and offered more salve for my multiple wounds. The food they fed me and the friendship they gave me nourished me at a soul level.

Word of my tragedy traveled quickly through my network of friends. I already had a half-dozen offers of places I could stay indefinitely until I could get my feet on the ground. Each time I stopped for a moment to consider the possibility of staying for more than a few days with one, a gust of wind would blow, and my ping pong ball would go flying to another place. I was unable to settle. Yet, in my constant bouncing from place to place and person to person, I discovered that my village was larger than I realized. Even people from my distant past time-traveled into my present.

"Teri, this is Pam Flood." The sweet high-pitched feminine voice reached out of the telephone through my ear canal and plucked several memory cords deep in the crevices of my brain. Pam's daughter, Heather, was my best friend from fourth through 12th grades. Pam was my second mother. When she called, I felt her fingers brushing my bangs out of my face (even though I hadn't had bangs in nearly 20 years). Her voice reached through the telephone lines with a Mommy-make-it-better kiss on the part of my hair.

I met Heather the first day of school of fourth grade. It was the first year I wasn't looking forward to going to school because that July no one came to my 10th birthday party. Heather was the new girl, and she invited me over to play after school. I never had a lonely birthday again.

True to their surname, Heather and Pam, flooded me with a sweet nectar of compliments every time I saw them. Nothing was spared a heartfelt compliment, my hair, my clothes, my ideas, even the things that I thought didn't warrant a compliment, like my braces and my glasses. If I paid them a compliment, it was always returned in triplicate. To this day, every time I am touched by their presence in my life, be it through a card or email, a telephone call, or a lunch date, I walk away feeling as though I have been baptized. I feel cleansed and pure, like their perception of me is so genuine and authentic that I cannot deny the raw essence of who I am. Their compliments and gifts wash away all that is not me. They carry these high-pitched feminine voices that speak in almost perpetual falsetto. Sometimes I wonder if most of their communication is in a tone imperceptible to the human ear, high pitched like a dog whistle, and carries a vibration that has a subtle yet undeniable effect on the human nervous system.

"Hi Pam. It's so good to hear from you." She couldn't begin to know how relieved I was to hear her voice. She had this ability to be present without hovering, and be available without smothering. She'd always have milk and cookies for us after school. If we wanted her to, she'd sit down and listen; and if we didn't want her, she wouldn't. She was the mother who listened to our grievances about life, but never gave advice unless we asked. She celebrated our triumphs, particularly the ones that no one else considered significant.

"Teri, you are one of the kindest people I've ever known. Thank you for saying that. How are you?" Those last three words that usually rattle out of someone's mouth automatically and unconsciously felt like rose petals that Pam placed gently and intentionally on my heart.

"Well, I've been better, but hearing from you really helps."

"Heather told me what you've been going through, I'm so sorry, Teri," she said my name like a familiar refrain to my favorite song. I

The Gift Inside the Wound

noted that she chose her words carefully, without mentioning Ted's name. She acknowledged my pain without naming it or giving power.

"Thank you." I didn't know what else to say.

"Listen Teri, I would really like to take you out to lunch. May I do that, Teri?" what she was really saying was *I'd like to nourish you, nurture you, love you, and nurse you into the full radiant being I know you to be.*

"I'd like that."

When we met a couple days later, Pam placed an envelope in front of me as we sat down at The Good Earth, a vegetarian friendly restaurant that held anchor in the Galleria mall for as long as I could remember. "Heather asked me to give you this."

The card was written in Heather's handwriting, a beautiful sweetness of compliments and support. Like her mother, Heather chose her words carefully, making sure to not mention the pain she knew I was feeling, but to emphasize the strength she knew I had inside me and the light she sees shine in me.

In true Flood fashion, tucked neatly inside the card was a gift certificate to Barnes and Noble. The gift card reached out from my past, triggering a multitude of memories of visiting libraries and bookstores with Heather, coming home with piles of books and working our way through them together, never talking about them, just reading them together side by side. Heather and I didn't ever need to talk about things, we just enjoyed sharing space with each other.

"I told her that I could pick it up for her," Pam continued, "but she insisted on going herself to get it. She left me with Baby Caitlin and ran to the store. She said she had to pick out the card herself."

I traced the edges of the gift card with my finger. Heather had only given birth to Caitlin a few days before she went to buy this for me. To leave her newborn and brave the cold was a sacrifice. I swallowed hard, accepting the medicine she offered me. The pill jagged going down, but I knew I needed its painkilling effects.

As Pam told the story, the medicine she and Heather gave me instantly began to work on my insides, like a hunger pain, but not. The new mother energy of Heather penetrated my belly to hug me from the inside. I knew she was probably the queen of nervous new mothers, so to leave her less than one-week-old baby with Grandma so that she could do something special for me in my time of pain was more than precious.

This gift carried more love with it than any gift I had ever received. Not because she had stressed about getting it. Not because she had put aside her nervousness about her daughter for me. Not because she made the trek to the store in the dead of winter so shortly after giving birth.

This gift seemed to reach out to me from the recesses of Heather's entire life and package up everything we had ever endured together. She was speaking to me from the dichotomy of labor pains to birthing bliss, of teenage angst to childhood joy, of fears and fantasies.

Heather was the oddball in class who wore dresses and didn't own a pair of jeans. I was the poor kid in class who wore hand-me-downs and garage sale clothes. We both had Coke-bottle glasses. She was the only person who could read more books than me. She was the smartest person in our class, and always broke the learning curve on tests. I was the weirdo who talked about auras and chakras and energies that no one else believed existed.

We were the misfits, the freaks in school who didn't fit the stereotypes of the rich Minneapolis suburban lifestyle. We were nerds together. In high school we joked that we would become either doctors, or lawyers, or Indian chiefs when we grew up. After college Heather went to medical school and became a pediatric hematologist, and I went through shamanic initiation and became a tribal elder. She became the doctor, and I became the Indian Chief.

Because we were so *not-normal*, Heather and I were often the recipients of bullying of various forms that were more often anonymous than blatant. We had a code of silence while handling these injustices, because to discuss the issues would give them more power. When we came home from a bike ride in sixth grade to find her garage covered in ketchup splatters, I just went to the back and hooked up the hose while she got a sponge. We worked together in silence to clean it up and never discussed it again. In ninth grade when I got assaulted at a football game, Heather escorted me to her dad's car and never asked me questions. She simply and firmly instructed her dad to just drive me home, giving him the message to honor our unwritten code. To speak about the pains we suffered would only perpetuate the trauma. Whatever wounds I experienced in Heather's presence never lasted long. It was like she and Pam taught me how to treat the wound like a chord that had been plucked on a piano with one note off. While the vibration may sound like fingernails on a chalkboard for a while, the sound will eventually die away if you don't touch the keys again. Instead, Pam and Heather always drowned out the bad sound by plucking more pleasant chords, those of genuine compliments, and continued playing the music of life as if the nasty chord was just a hiccup, forgotten as quickly as it struck.

While Heather and I learned to use silence as a mute button on bitterness, we also learned that words and language are often insufficient forms of communication, and that like in music, the pause in the action, the silence is more powerful than the sound. While we were generous with compliments to each other, we were very careful not to ever use words or language to try to define our relationship or our feelings for each other. We never really said "I love you" to each other, or used other terminology to define our relationship because it would only define and limit the potential. It was as if we understood that to leave some things unspoken between us was to allow access to the mystery and spaciousness of our connection. When we lost touch for several years after college, we never really missed each other because that undefined space was always there. We'd learned the spaciousness by spending hours reading in silence next to each other, or playing side by side building homes and structures with Legos, only speaking enough to ask one to pass a particular piece to the other. We shared space and allowed the invisible energies to work between us.

Perhaps because we knew the power of silence and invisible energies of the world, we developed a keen skill in observation, particularly of the "cool kids" who were often the perpetrators of our bullying. As a form of protection from the more blatant bullying we watched occur to less silent *not-normals* of school, Heather and I learned to wear invisibility cloaks as a means of avoiding the bullying as well as a means of observing and analyzing human behavior. Most of the time, the "cool kids" didn't even acknowledge that we existed. The arrogant computer geeks who proclaimed superiority by flaunting their smarts were the ones whose backpacks were "accidentally" snagged and pulled off and dumped out in the cafeteria garbage. Not us.

Heather and I pulled our invisibility hoods higher over our heads and wondered how people can be so mean. We kept to ourselves and listened quietly to the backstabbing rumors and heart-penetrating insults that were slung among "friends" in the hallways at school.

Heather and Pam are extensions of each other. While Pam mothers everyone she meets, Heather became a pediatric hematologist, a mother to children suffering blood disorders, giving her the opportunity to mother both the children and the parents through trauma. While I've never witnessed her at work, I have been the recipient of her doctoring on many occasions.

After lunch, Pam secured her purse high up on her shoulder to free up both her hands to take both my hands in hers. Her fingers were soft, yet her grip was firm and embracing.

"Teri, I want you to know, really know, that no matter what happens to you in your life, no matter where you go and what you do, no matter who you encounter and how they treat you, Teri, you are loved. You have to KNOW that you are loved. You must know this."

She didn't say "I love you" but she said "you are loved," leaving space for a greater energy. Through her hands and her words, Pam gave me an IV drip of healing medicine I couldn't refuse or deny. I felt it warm every part of me from the inside out.

After we parted, I walked straight to Barnes and Noble at the end of the mall and purchased a leather bound journal with the gift card Heather had given me. Before leaving the store, I found a cozy chair and wrapped myself in my invisibility cloak and tuned into the silence. I turned to the front page and wrote in the center of the page:

"The wound is the place where the light enters you." ~Rumi

The Gift Inside the Wound

Cleaning the Wound ~ Letting Go

Teri Leigh

The Gift Inside the Wound

Grief's Grip On My Throat

*"There is a sacredness in tears.
They are not the mark of weakness, but of power."*
~Washington Irving

After bouncing around from guest bed to guest bed for nearly a week, friends offered me their Northern Minnesota cabin. The thought of nestling into a Northwoods cabin for a solid week felt really nice.

After swallowing Heather's medicine and letting Pam's IV drip, I was beginning to feel a little bit more human. It was time to look at my wounds myself and start the process of washing them clean.

Besides, I had told the story of what happened so many times that my throat was feeling raw. The introvert in me was craving alone time. I wanted to cry alone, to wash my gashes and lacerations with my salt water tears, by myself.

I thought I was no stranger to Grief. I had lived through clinical depression, survived the failure of a business, beaten life-threatening allergies, and navigated unemployment. I thought I had beaten Grief to a pulp over years of punching and jabbing at him at every turn, mostly in cardio-kickboxing classes. The truth was that Grief was impervious to my abuse, able to duck and dodge every blow I threw. He took residence in corners of my body waiting patiently for me to realize that he wasn't meant to be beaten, but rather, befriended.

On Fuck You Sunday, Grief came at me in full force. He wasn't going to dodge me this time. Instead, He attacked. I saw him coming. Unable to bob and weave or duck and cover, and knowing he wouldn't greet me kindly this time, I took his blow. He plowed into me and knocked me out. As I accepted the kind offers of many first responders who picked me up, carried me, and let me limp along while draping my arms over their shoulders, Grief waited patiently; always in the shadows, but always there.

But now, I felt stronger. I was ready. When Grief offered me his weathered knobby hand and invited me to spend a week alone with him at a Northwoods Minnesota cabin in winter, I accepted.

Damn, his hand was cold.

On the way to the cabin, I stopped to visit my oldest living relative, my great Aunt T, who was about to celebrate 100 laps around the sun. The last year had been hard on Aunt T. Grief had been a constant companion to her for the duration of her most recent sun lap. Her favorite nephew, the son she never had, had taken ill and passed suddenly that fall. A month later, a doctor told her that she needed a double hip replacement, but no surgeon would perform the procedure due to her advanced age. She was forced to give up her bi-weekly swimming trips to the neighborhood Super 8 Motel with her friends. She sold her car and depended upon the goodwill of neighbors and in-home care nurses.

In hugging her hello, she felt half the size from the last time I had seen her. When I commented about her nearing her 100th birthday she giggled and said, "if I make it that long."

Looking in her eyes, I could tell that, like my mother, she had made friends with Grief. I knew this could likely be the last time I'd see her before placing a flower on her grave.

Grief gave me a good-old-boys-slap on the back as if to say, "We're just getting started!"

As I drove away crying, I didn't bother to wipe the tears away anymore. If I was going to get reacquainted with Grief, I figured he'd want me to speak his language.

Opening the door to the cabin felt like ripping off the initial bandages from my wounds. The sound of the door across the floor scratched at my ears as if the gauze ripped the hair from my skin. The musty, closed-up cabin smell hit me like the stench of dried blood left too long under soaked bandages.

I took two steps into the cabin, collapsed to the floor and let myself cry.

The Gift Inside the Wound

The echoes of the empty cabin made harmony with the murmurs of sobs still ricocheting around inside the hollow walls of my chest. The salty tears stung. Every once in a while a blubber or whelp cracked out of my throat, and another clump of puss and blood dislodged, re-exposing the wound.

The tears flowed heavily, freely, like a leaky faucet gone way beyond a simple drip. Everything in me felt as dank and empty and cold as the cabin. I didn't bother to wipe the tears, or the snot. I just let them blubber out of me, all over my puffy purple down jacket.

I lost time again. The empty silence of the cabin muffled my ability to hear. In a tiny moment, a breath between sobs, I caught a glimpse of myself in the front hall mirror. The scene looked like a television on mute.

"Television dramas played on mute turn into comedies," I heard Grandpa's voice inside my head. While I'd never heard him say that when he was alive, it sounded like something he would say.

And, just like that, comforted by Grandpa's presence, my tears cartwheeled from sadness into laughter. I gathered myself up off the floor and went about the task of unpacking.

Grandpa always loved to joke. While practical jokes were his favorite, he was a master at finding intelligent humor in any situation. Of course, I didn't know this while Grandpa was alive. To me, he was an avid reader, and a grouchy old man who got annoyed when I interrupted his afternoon nap or dog-eared the pages of his books. I only met my Grandpa as someone I enjoyed well after his death, when I attended a shamanic grief ritual on my 37th birthday, two years prior to Fuck You Sunday. I attended the ritual with the intention of grieving my grandmother's death from the Christmas before, but found myself grieving much more, and developing a new relationship with my maternal Grandpa Edgar and my paternal Grandma Alice.

At first the ritual process felt completely foreign and rather stilted to me. While a group of people danced around a fire chanting to African rhythms, we were invited to kneel and cry at this elaborate shrine built of leaves and twigs and flowers and vines. How was I supposed to MAKE myself cry? It felt so, well, fake.

But within just minutes after the initial prayer invocation, I felt this undeniable pull towards the grief shrine. As if under some sort of spell, my legs danced their way closer and closer to the shrine and my chanting grew softer and softer until eventually I was sitting at the ground in front of the shrine barely whispering the chant.

Within seconds of sitting down, I felt a cry-lump in my throat that couldn't be swallowed. Then, I felt someone's violent hands at my neck, squeezing. The hands were not human, they were long and bony, like a character out of a Tim Burton animation. These were the hands of Grief. His thumbs pressed firmly into my soft flesh just above my clavicle. The fingers wrapped around and clutched menacingly to the vertebrae of my neck. As these hands squeezed, the bubble at my throat only grew. A fiery liquid oozed down my spinal cord and slithered itself around my internal organs at the same time as the bubble at my throat pushed itself through to the back of my tongue and the roof of my mouth.

Then it happened: a deep loud guttural inhuman sound exploded out of my mouth. At the same time, my body collapsed into uncontrollable spasms. My face planted in the dirt, and my lungs emptied into a wail that left a puddle of snot and saliva and even a little blood mixed into the earth that smeared across my face.

At first I thought I was crying about Grandma's Christmas Day death. Then, I found myself sobbing for the death of my grandfather, and for missing his funeral while backpacking through Europe. And then I cried that I inherited my grandfather's car after that trip. And I cried for that car, which I had named Grandpa, which also died prematurely and unexpectedly. And then, I cried because I never met my paternal grandparents because they both died before I was born.

And then I cried over the cookie that my brother stole from me and taunted me about when I was six. . . and a birthday party that none of my friends showed up to when I was 10. . . And then I cried because I had so much to cry about and because the things that made me cry were so stupid.

And then, suddenly, and oddly, my crying turned into laughing. Laugh-crying, or cry-laughing. I wasn't sure. I laughed because I was crying so hard. And then, I couldn't tell if I was crying or laughing or both. I laughed like my Grandpa Edgar used to laugh. And I cried like my Grandma Alice used to cry.

Then suddenly, I didn't miss Grandpa anymore. And I didn't feel bad that I'd never met Grandma Alice. As I cry-laughed with my entire body kneeling at the grief shrine, I realized they hadn't really gone anywhere. They didn't "die." They lived on, inside me. Their blood, their energy, their spirits coursed through my veins. When that thought hit me, Grief's grip around my throat released.

His hand freed from my neck, he offered it to lift me up off the soil. I took it and thanked him. That day, I shook hands with Grief for the first time. We made a pact. I agreed to welcome him like a friend next time he came around, and he agreed to only come knocking for the big stuff. I figured I had paid my Grief dues and was good for a while. Until someday. The day I walked into the Northwoods cabin, I knew I couldn't buy more time against someday.

Grief doesn't keep time.

After unpacking, I let my dog Sukha lead me on a long walk across the frozen lake. The blanket of snow was just over ankle deep, and Sukha hopped like a doe through the powder that absorbed every sound. Naked trees lined the edges of the lake, and the clear blue sky invited me into white silence. The white nothingness, and the bitter cold invited reflections of the vacuum inside my chest.

A few footprints and snowmobile tracks criss-crossed the lake but left no clear path to follow. Lost and directionless in wide open space, I followed Sukha, who relished the freedom off her leash.

The reflection of the sun off the snow was so bright it hurt my eyes. Winter bit my tears, sending microscopic ice chips through my tear ducts into the center of my skull. The bitter cold froze the surface of my heart just enough for me to crave the softness inside it, like frostbite.

An hour later, shivering and cold-bitten, I stoked a fire in the great room of the cabin. The smoke and warmth felt more nourishing to me than food. The constant movement of the flames found a CPR rhythm. Each time I thought my heart might stop from the stabbing pain of Grief, the fire would crackle a loud pop. I fell asleep to the sad lullaby of the fire, its pacemaker attached to my heart.

The next morning, I received an email from Ted, his first communication to me since Fuck You Sunday. I read it several times through, each time, the words went through my eyes, and knotted themselves up inside my skull. More of his words slithered and twisted their way down my tear ducts, burning salt down my face. The rest of them dripped down my sinus cavity, oozing their way through the column of my throat into my gut. There they wrapped my vital organs into tight knots that couldn't be untangled with even the deepest of breath.

If the letter had been on paper, I would have torn it up into tiny pieces and thrown it into the fire. Ted's words felt colder than the bitter Minnesota wind, and I thought that maybe if I burned it I could find some warmth inside them. But, the letter was just words on my phone, so instead, I wanted the fire to burn the shell of me that remained. For several hours, I let the heat consume me. I danced with the urge to climb in and let myself be burned like a witch at the stake.

Then, I prayed.

While I was no stranger to prayer, it was something I usually did on my yoga mat, on my meditation cushion, or in front of my ancestor shrine. I hadn't actually ever gotten down on my knees, folded my hands and prayed.

When I started speaking, Sukha left her perch on the couch and sat down next to me as if I were talking to her. So I directed my prayers to her. Awkwardly, I asked her to keep me safe and show me the way through this nasty forest. I asked her to give me glimmers of light along the way. Her soft brown eyes gazed adoringly into mine.

Breath escaped me as I felt Grief's grip around my throat. The lump of my pain was squeezed out of my mouth like toothpaste, my words felt thick on my tongue. The more Grief squeezed my throat, the emptier my chest felt, and the louder the words banged around inside, like a softball in a clothes dryer. My prayer turned to screams. Piercing, guttural, knifing screams that reached down into my gut and hacked away at the knots of my internal organs. With each wail, Sukha raised a paw and scratched at my chest. Her claws ripped at my heart, and the pain only made me wail louder.

Then, like the buzzer on the softball filled clothes dryer, one low bone rattling vocalization escaped my lips…and then, silence. Sukha curled her fox-like body into a ball next to me and filled the silence with one long sighing exhale followed by sweet puppy purrs. I curled my broken body around her on the stone hearth of the fireplace and fell asleep.

The next morning, as I had nearly every day for over a decade, I crawled onto my yoga mat and continued my prayer from the night before. Using my body as my vocal chords, my prayer was more articulate.

Through sun salutations, I asked for the strength and guidance to know what to do next and to take that step. I felt old and decrepit, broken and beaten, but the movement and breath pushed life force into my vital organs. Although I felt like I was standing up for the first time in several days I continued to move and breathe, from one pose to the next, trusting the muscle memory of my legs and core to step me from down dog into warriors. I felt muscles stretch in my hips and shoulders and chest and back that I didn't know I had.

I felt as though the spirit that inhabits my body had outgrown my tissues and was tugging and pulling at the muscles and tendons begging them to expand to fit its new size and shape. While the postures were familiar and I could rely on the intelligence of years of practice, my center of gravity had entirely shifted. I needed to find a new state of balance in every pose.

Under the pain, there was a peace, like the quietude of the frozen lake. Each night, I found myself humbled, on my knees, in front of the fire, my head bowed and tears streaming down my cheeks. By morning, the fire had melted those bitter-cold tears of sorrow, anger, and fear into drops of gratitude, joy, and even love.

My last morning at the cabin, I felt like I had washed away the chunkiest debris from all my wounds. I took my last walk on the lake.

"You're doing the impossible," Grandpa Edgar whispered in my head as I looked back at the house in the distance. "You're walking on water."

Teri Leigh

Sweating Out the Tears

"The cure for anything is salt water: sweat, tears, and the sea."
~Isak Dinesen

As I packed up the car to leave the Northwoods cabin, Grief buckled himself into the passenger seat of my car while Sukha settled herself into the back seat. I had to bring her back to Ted's house, at least for the time being. My life with Ted in our house was over. It was now Ted's house. For the first time in my life, I had no home to go to. Ted's letter offered me $5000 if I would sign a quit claim deed to the house and walk away. I knew I needed to consult a divorce lawyer before I agreed to anything. But I couldn't really think about that. I had to think about where I would sleep tonight, and tomorrow, and the next night.

Somehow, in the more lucid moments between crying spells and treks across the icy lake, I managed to work enough to book a number of business events. I reached out to my nationwide network of friends and angels and business contacts. I booked myself on an extended road trip, a nationwide tour.

Via text, Ted and I agreed that he would watch Sukha until I returned in May. We both agreed that we hoped to have divorce papers ready to sign by then. I dropped Sukha off at the house while Ted was away at school. I cried, promising her I would never leave her again.

Grief stayed pretty quiet as a passenger on the drive to Sioux Falls. He was patient, knowing that my favorite place to process pain is on my yoga mat. He let me teach, without interruption, to an eager crew of students in Sioux Falls. But on my last day of a three-day weekend event, after my teaching was done, when I finally surrendered to my mat in a Bikram Yoga class, Grief reminded me that I had not left him in the north woods cabin fireplace cinders.

During that hot yoga class, he sucker-punched me in the gut and pushed the tears not only out my mouth and eyes, but out of every pore of my skin. For over a decade, my yoga mat had been my happy place. That day, it was a place of devastation.

Twelve years earlier, I took my first Bikram class in hopes of building flexibility to enhance my kickboxing and balance my weight-training. The 110° room with 70% humidity reminded me of the time my older brother taunted me by putting his sweaty hockey socks over my nose and holding me down to the ground until our mother told him to leave me alone.

The sense of smell and memory are deeply connected. The neurological pathways from the nose lead to the part of the brain that house the memory banks. The class itself was like a good taunting from my brother.

But I was too distracted by the auras and visions I saw in the mirror to care. All my life I have been able to see auras, colors and lights shimmering off of people's bodies. Most of the time, I don't pay attention, treating them as annoying holographic disruptions in my field of vision.

As a child I used to play "what color is that person?" games with my dad in the grocery store and during the boring sermons at church, but once I got to college I trained my eyes to not pay much attention. I downplayed my skill with others by saying that I saw auras like they see what people are wearing. While it can give some cues to people's moods and personalities, for the most part, I didn't pay attention or care.

In that first Bikram Yoga class the mirrors lit up to me like a laser light show combined with a fireworks display, and I couldn't help but pay attention. I saw the significant shifts and changes that occurred when people put themselves into these yoga positions.

It was the first time I had ever seen an aura in a mirror, and more importantly, it was the first time I'd ever seen my own aura. Something about the first breathing exercise of tilting my head back and forward with pressure under my chin had activated my third eye so that I could see in ways I had never seen before. I started taking classes every day, not to better my body or improve my mental clarity, but to watch the light show and study the effects of the postures on the bodies in the room.

Like my menacing older brother, Bikram teachers are ruthless. They teach discipline, speaking a precise dialogue from a pedestal at the front of the room where they keep a vigilant eye on their students, quick to reprimand and correct. I learned the rules quickly so that I could keep in the good graces of the instructor while I conducted my own aura research. All my talents of being the good student came into play as I learned to not drink water unless instructed to do so, not wipe my face of the sweat, and never ever adjust my clothing.

I even became a master at pretending to look at my own eyes in the mirror, which worked well because, for me, auras and colors are more visible in my peripheral and inner vision than when I look directly.

I met Ted in a Bikram Yoga class. On our first date, at brunch after a Bikram Yoga class, Ted asked me why I was here on earth, what I thought was the meaning of life.

I told him that I wanted to be like Henry David Thoreau, that I wanted to suck up all the marrow of life. I said that I wanted to experience every human emotion the body could handle, to know each sensation in my bones and feel them to the fullest and not just the good ones. I wanted to feel love in the same fullness and capacity as I feel grief because the two emotions mirror each other. In the grief of loss one can fully acknowledge and know the depth of love. Without grief, love cannot be fully known. I remember being impressed with myself in my answer, and really believing it at the time.

At that time, when I first discovered yoga, I hadn't yet met and shook hands with Grief. I'd avoided him by becoming a master at ducking and dodging, bobbing and weaving, punching and jabbing anything and everything that offered the tiniest hints of Grief in my life.

Now that Grief had me by the wrists and throat, I wanted to take my words back. In saying them to Ted that day, had I set a self-fulfilling prophecy for myself? If living life to the fullest meant feeling Grief this deep, perhaps I didn't want it anymore. Could I please just go back to blissful ignorance? Maybe the roots of my words were still attached to the taste buds on my tongue. Couldn't I just suck them back in like a long strand of spaghetti?

I hadn't been to a Bikram class in five years. I had long since switched my research from the stagnant and consistent practice of 26 repeated postures to the more fluid and variable practice of vinyasa flow. My study had flipped from observing effects on students in classes I was taking to observing the effects on students in classes I was teaching. Most of the classes I took didn't have mirrors, and I had learned to turn off my vision in order to get into my own practice.

Stepping into that Sioux Falls hot class, I faced a mirror at a time in my life when I wasn't sure I wanted to see my own aura, as raw and wounded as I was, reflecting the still open sores of Fuck You Sunday and subsequent interactions with Grief. The instructor began, and his voice sounded uncannily like my menacing and taunting older brother. I was 12 years old again, feeling not good enough, and hating the image of myself in the mirror.

"INHALE, YOUR ARMS UP OVER YOUR HEAD!"

I couldn't ignore the energy laser light show bouncing around the room. As the instructor barked orders, tiny energy spears sparked from his mouth. Each syllable, a spear pierced a pore of my skin, ripping a tiny little cut into my being. These tiny holes filled with sweat. Each puddle of sweat carried the toxicity of some memory. Not just those from Fuck You Sunday, but from the entire decade of my marriage, and the three decades before that. Every drop of sweat also carried the salt that made each sore sting.

"INTERLACE YOUR FINGERS!"

He offered no respite between directions. Periods and commas and other punctuation were too cumbersome. The attack of syllables shot out like machine gun fire. I closed my eyes and hummed "sticks and stones will break my bones, but words . . ."

"OPEN YOUR EYES! LOOK AT YOURSELF IN THE MIRROR."

Fuck, he saw me.

My mantra wasn't any more effective here than it was when I was bullied during recess in the third grade. In a quick glance, I could've sworn the instructor was Ted wearing some kind of Scooby Doo mask, and the only words coming out of his mouth were "Fuck You." I felt every single syllable of every instruction pierce my skin and rip at the soft tissue underneath.

Fuck you…
Fuck you…
Fuck you…
Fuck you…

"RELEASE YOUR INDEX FINGERS!"

Every student in the room became a human energy gun, pointing their weapons at the ceiling. Their own angsts and toxins and pains and fumblings and fears and fuck-yous laser-lighted through their finger-guns to the ceiling.

The ceiling taunted me, "I'm rubber and you're glue, what you shoot bounces off of me and sticks to you."

Tiny spears and daggers of energy-light rained down the room as toxic sweat-lava dribbled down my body. Red-hot trickles became fiery streams of slow-moving lava that burned into my skin and revealed the raw underneath, like poking holes in a paper lantern to reveal more of the light. The vulnerable essence of myself squinted at the vast openness that existed outside my body. It's really scary out there!

"PULL YOUR ARMS BEHIND YOUR EARS!"

There it was, the one I knew was coming. The one instruction I couldn't follow. One reason I traded Bikram for vinyasa was because my shoulders wouldn't let me pull my arms behind my ears. No matter how hard I pushed and tried and adjusted, I could never get my arms behind my ears. They just didn't go there. In that moment, my shoulders locked into place, and right there in the mirror, I watched my own aura melt into a salty puddle at my feet. In the mirror, the image of my body looked like it was rendered by a carnival mirror.

"NEW GIRL IN THE RED PANTS, PULL YOUR ARMS BEHIND YOUR EARS!"

The instructor singled me out. In that moment, I was a nobody who couldn't follow one simple instruction. My years of practice and training melted at my feet. His words came down on me like a chainsaw and splattered chunks of me all over the room.

I spent the rest of the class in a dissociative state. When I didn't sleepwalk through a pose or sequence, some memory from my past would merge with the present moment and take me through the pose in a sort of alternate universe. The word "change" out of the teacher's mouth triggered a quantum leap into another time, another world, or into a silent and empty zoned-out space.

"CHANGE"

The teacher's voice morphed into a Charlie Brown cartoon teacher's unintelligible muttering while I half stepped into straddle forward fold with my hands clasped behind my back. Big plopping tears oozed from my eyes like a leaky faucet onto the mat below. I opened my mouth and saltwater mixed with snot drooled onto my yoga mat out of my eyes and nose and mouth.

"CHANGE"

Rabbit Pose. I wanted to scratch, dig, and burrow. Curled up into a ball of myself, I wanted to rip into my skin and peel off all the layers that Ted had ever touched. I wanted to take an eraser to my insides and erase every cell, every memory, every sensation of him. If I could erase it all, could I get a do-over? If I rejected everything I had ever accepted from him and about him and drank scalding water to burn out the residue from the inside out, could I start over fresh and clean? I wanted no part of the emptiness in my being. I pounded the floor in my sobs, and then scratched at the skin on my face and arms and legs.

"CHANGE"

The Gift Inside the Wound

Seated Twist. The spot at the back of my shoulder blades was so exposed, and it was the one place on my entire body that I could not protect. I couldn't cover it with the palm of my hand. I simply couldn't reach it. So I thought maybe I could squeeze it from the inside through my twist. I twisted further, deeper, knotting my arms through my legs and squeezing with all my might.

It felt like a complex knot of silk gauze about the size of a golf ball. In some places it was slippery and in some places it was sticky. Parts of the silk had never been exposed to the world, protected by the knots and folds. Inside those folds was a gift, a precious gem, like the center of a Tootsie Pop.

Maybe, just maybe, if I squeezed enough, when I unwound the pose, the layers of the silk would peel away. All the stained and dirties and sullied parts of my past would fall away. Maybe then I could enjoy the full flavor of the Tootsie Pop's chewy chocolate center. But the process of unraveling the silk was like licking the shards of the Tootsie Pop, piercing splinters in my tongue. Each loosening fold of the silk sent shattering pain to the center of the gem inside me. The silk was my protective wrapping.

I wanted to touch the brilliance of the multi-faceted kaleidoscopic gem. Of course it wouldn't let me so close so easy. Strength comes from feeling the pain necessary to excavate the wound and reveal the gift.

"CHANGE"

Breath of Fire. If feeling the pain, all of it, feeling it completely is what it takes to excavate the wounds, I wanted to feel it. I wanted to feel it all. I shape-shifted into a fire-breathing dragon, and exhaled bursts of flames, piercing the air with my wrath and determination, and every ounce of pain I had ever felt in my entire life.

"CHANGE"

Corpse Pose. To be reborn, I must die. I collapsed. I surrendered. I merged with the sweaty-sock-smelling-fungus-infected carpet.

Just when I thought I was done, cooked, burnt to a black charred crisp, I looked up through the wetness of sweaty tears from between the fibers of the carpet to see Grief smiling. His wretched and wrinkled hand reached down to me. I took his hand, and he hoisted my sweaty salty teardrop body into his arms.

Even Grief has a heart.

Making Friends with Grief

"To weep is to make less the depth of grief."
~William Shakespeare

The next morning, I took a yoga class from my favorite teacher, Elizabeth, who had come to Sioux Falls from Boston to teach a workshop in conjunction with the one I led. Elizabeth came around to assist me, in straddle forward fold with my hands clasped behind my back. One of the most vulnerable positions of the class, upside down with my legs apart, my hands tied behind my back, my heart was fully exposed. She identified Ted's "fuck you" knife protruding from the middle of my back. She inserted her skillful fingers in and around my shoulder blades and manipulated just enough to crack my breastbone. She kneaded at the tip of the knife, squeezing it to the surface from the inside out. The release of the knife gave space for Grief's hand to squeeze my heart in a way he couldn't reach before. Together, he and Elizabeth squeezed, and I openly drooled tears onto my yoga mat, and wondered how long it would be before I had a day without tears?

Evidently not today. I had more crud to clean out of my wounds.

After class, weather reports showed a winter storm coming through South Dakota and Iowa. I packed up quickly, hoping to outrun it. My heated seats felt like a warm hug. Driving was treacherous, to say the least. I went from icy fog to sleeting rain to cottonball snowflakes over the course of one hour. In what seemed like no time, it was dark.

I hate driving in the dark. The laser that shaved my eyesight back from nearly blind to 20/20 in my late 20s made my vision tender. The reflections of light off puddles in the pavement and halos from headlights stung my irises. Each rain droplet that landed on my windshield reflected the light of headlights and tail lights into a kaleidoscope of refractions. While beautiful, it was so distracting that staying between the white and yellow lines of the road required intense focus. The reflective letters of the street signs. The red tail lights of the cars in front of me. The white headlights of the cars behind me, in my side and rearview mirrors. The droplets of sleet and rain reflecting lights on my windshield. The puddles on the pavement. The extra bright lights bounced off the wet pavement and shimmered like a mermaid's tail. Everywhere I looked, bright blinding light flashed against black emptiness.

It was beautiful, and terrifying.

Exhausted from crying on my yoga mat that morning and driving through Iowa on a January evening in freezing rain, I was 16 steps beyond miserable. I turned up the heat in my car to 75 degrees and put the seat warmer on full blast. I admitted defeat and stopped at the next hotel somewhere between Nowhere and Nothingness, somewhere amidst the corn fields of Iowa.

When I got out of the car, the sky cried big heavy faucet drops of tears. Stunned, I stood still in the rain, letting the skies waters blend with my eye waters. My emotional pain festered and bubbled like vinegar poured on baking soda. I wanted to suck the water into chest and feel the effervescent sting where it hurt the most – my heart. I took a deep breath and choked. My coughing snapped me out of the rain trance, and I allowed Grief to lead me by the hand into the $59/night Iowa hotel.

I didn't pay much attention to the clerk behind the counter. I just wanted to get into my room and pretend the rest of the world didn't exist. I didn't have anything in me for even the most mundane of engagements with other people.

The hotel clerk couldn't have been more than 22 years old. When she gave me my room key, instead of just sliding it across the counter, she handed it to me, and grabbed my hand with her other hand.

The Gift Inside the Wound

"Smile," she said, "I know it feels fake, but I just saw this video that said that if you fake smile, the muscles in your face tell your brain to make you feel happy for real. It can't hurt." She looked me right in the eye and winked before she let go of my hand. Her smile traveled down her arms, through my hands, and emerged on my own lips.

"Thank you," I whispered, swallowing back the sob at the back of my throat, realizing that I couldn't tell if the wetness on my face was leftover rain, or fresh tears. I didn't care. Thankfully, neither did she.

Once locked safely in my room, I collapsed in child's pose on my yoga mat in the space between the bathroom and the entry door. The groan of the room heater rattled a menacing growl. Despite using my puffy down jacket as my tortoise shell, the heat monster's voice penetrated my pores and awoke something inside my gut. I let out the guttural wail that had been brewing inside my belly. The sobbing quivers of my body argued with the rattles from the heater, each trying to be louder than the other.

The cavernous sinus space in the center of my skull where all the five senses merge, flooded. It started with a little knot the size of a baby brussel sprout. It pushed itself up from my heart to my throat and put pressure on the back of my nose. That knot then squeezed little pocket nodes to fill juices into the empty space. It got warm and melted everything on the inside. Eventually, all the emotions poured out, first through my pores, then through my nose, and finally through my eyes. It was a dense and heavy substance, sensitive and palpable.

This time, I welcomed the release. Grief brought his friend, Intuition. Emotion is the language of intuition. Together, Emotion and Intuition reside in the same space in my body, that empty cavernous space of my sinuses. My five senses merged into one. Inside the sinus cavity, where the eye ducts, ear canals, nasal passage and throat connect is the place where the neurological messages mix and process information in the space of intuition and instinct…my sixth sense.

And when Intuition spoke, her message was as bright and blinding as the refractions of light through my windshield. *"Jump"* she whispered, in a loud penetrating whisper that blew like a fan through the whole inside of my head. Suddenly, the words "do not walk outside this area" on the wing of my symbolic airplane felt too confining.

Deep breath…and I fell off the wing.
I woke up the next morning, feeling clean.

Later the next day, while passing through Indiana, I stopped at my friend Amy's place. She was one of my bridesmaids, whose signature sealed my marriage license. I took off my wedding ring and wrapped it in a pair of socks. I asked her to keep it for me until I decided what to do with it.

I was a single woman again.

Somewhere around the Georgia-Florida border, I received word that one of the two events I had scheduled in Florida hadn't reached minimum capacity and was canceled. Without this contract, my trip to Florida would barely break even financially.
Had I mis-read Intuition's message? She clearly told me to jump, and trust the process. Letting go of Ted was one thing, but letting go of my career at the same time was like letting go of the rope with BOTH hands.
Grief was there for his karmic paycheck, and I owed him a large balloon payment. That balloon payment, letting go of my career, that was a price steeper than I was comfortable paying.

Exactly one month after Fuck You Sunday, I crossed over another comfort zone threshold. This time I was more than pushed or swiped or swept out of my comfort zone. I was BLASTED. I knew I couldn't drive back over the center line rumble strips. No, this threshold had the spikes on the ground that would flatten my tires. Evidently, inviting Grief to be my friend meant that I couldn't turn back.

Fine, if I can't beat him, I might as well join him.

I pulled off the highway, turned the hazard lights on my car, and let Grief take me full throttle once again. I kicked my feet on the floor, as if I was trying to modify my vehicle Fred Flintstone style. I banged on the steering wheel, and screamed so loud one of the windows might have cracked.

Twenty minutes passed. Maybe longer.

Then, like a jaded member of a bomb squad who just deactivated a pipe bomb, I wiped my snotty nose on my sleeve, turned off the hazard lights, flipped my turn signal and rejoined the flow of traffic.

An hour later, I sat down in a northern Florida Waffle House, the only customer in the restaurant.

"Honey, what can I get you? Looks like you've had a bear of a day," the waitress's southern charm and accent was like a soothing pain killer. I relaxed in her presence, and almost instantly felt better. Grief walked in behind me, sat at a corner booth at the opposite end of the restaurant and winked at me.

"Just give me what he loves to cook the most."

I didn't care what I ate, I just wanted to be nourished by someone who was feeling something different than what I had just felt inside the cavern in my skull.

"You got it, Sugar."

When she put the plate of over easy eggs she also pushed a Dove chocolate wrapper my way. "I think you need this more than I do."

The wrapper read: Be free. Be happy. Be you.

"Yes. Thank you." I whispered, and taped it inside my journal.

The next afternoon, I found myself on a stand-up-paddle board on Lake Minnehaha, the laughing waters, in Clermont, FL. In Minneapolis where I had spent most of my life there is Minnehaha Creek and Minnehaha Falls, and here I come all the way to Florida to stand-up paddleboard on Minnehaha Lake.

My yoga body and inner sense of balance coupled with my high school years of synchronized swimming allowed me to adapt well to standing on a paddleboard on a calm lake. I remembered how to dance with the water instead of against it. Like I had when I walked across the frozen lake in Minnesota, once again, Grandpa knocked inside my skull

"You're walking on water."

The paddle in my hands was another story. I have never been good with equipment. While I know instinctively how to reach out and grab a fistful of water and pull it like a handlebar to maneuver my way through fluid, to grab the water with a paddle just didn't work as nicely for me. I had good balance, and I could calibrate and tune and adjust the deep inner muscles of my core to compensate for the subtle and dramatic shifts of my foundation.

But, I could not steer.

I laughed loudly with the lapping waters of Lake Minnehaha when I saw Grief sitting on the dock. There were others too, several others, sitting with him, dangling their feet in the lake. Together, they were my Spirit team. My fate was in their hands now. I needed only keep balance as I surrendered steering to them.

Stitching the Wound ~ Feeling Strong

Teri Leigh

Whatever Makes You Happy. Do That.

"Ever since happiness heard your name, it has been running through the streets trying to find you."
Hafiz

Grief squeezed tears from my eyes and poured them over my wounds time and again. My wounds needed stitches, but first, I needed to make peace with Vulnerability, Grief's twin brother. Fortunately, my next stop in Florida was a long weekend with my friend Eddie, a transgender man who embraced Vulnerability as his guardian angel when he went through his transition.

Eddie opened the door and welcomed me into his arms. Four cats peered at me from the various perches and hiding spots around the living room. His embrace was warm, and inviting, a soothing salve to the sting of my recent salt water tears.

As Facebook friends we had never actually met in person. But that night, sitting around his backyard fire pit with Vulnerability planted in the empty space between us, we talked as if we were old friends catching up after 20 years apart. We shared stories with as much animation and excitement as the flames enjoyed licking the air.

I spoke of my transition from marriage to divorce, and tears wet my cheeks once again. But this time my tears didn't sting, they soothed. I found myself gushing my story in a way I hadn't with any of my other friends, sharing a rawness with Eddie that I hadn't even been able to admit to myself before. In the presence of a man who had survived a bigger transition than I could ever imagine, I felt safe enough to be completely vulnerable. For the first time since Ted's first Fuck You, I honestly thought everything could eventually be okay.

When I looked up at Eddie after telling my story, I saw the same crew of angels that had sat with Grief on the dock. Vulnerability and Hope, Transition and Protection, and several others had all pulled up chairs around the fire. They all heard me, and were ready and waiting to stitch me up.

As a transgender bisexual man, Eddie walked hand in hand with Transition every single day of his life. He skillfully validated my struggles of transitioning from married to divorced without diminishing my process even though it was far less intense than his own transition from female to male.

While the light of our conversation never flickered , our yawns grew wider and my early morning teaching schedule required that we douse the flames and let our stories serve as warming embers to slumber. While I felt completely safe with Eddie, I feared his cats' dander would bite and claw at my lungs, tightening my already constricted heart.

"I gotta admit. I'm more than a little scared to go inside the house for the night," I told Eddie as he started to smother the fire with earth. While I've never been afraid of needles at the doctor's office, I most certainly am afraid of a cat's claws.

"Why's that?"

"I used to be deathly allergic to cats."

"Used to be is the operative phrase there," Eddie suggested. "What happened?"

"After one night at a friend's house with a cat, I suffered chronic bronchitis for over 18 months, resulting in several hospital emergency room visits to clear my airways. In my last week in the dorms, just as my breathing function was beginning to return to normal again, a freshman brought a kitten into her dorm room on the first floor of my building. All the way up on the third floor, not 10 minutes later, my lungs detected the cat dander, and I wheezed. I spent the next several hours in the ER, and the next several months with chronic bronchitis once again.

"My allergy doctor said that my case was the most severe he had ever seen in his 30-year career. Allergy shots could cause more harm than good. The inhalers and nebulizers I tried gave me heart palpitations, and each allergy medication had some weird and unique side effect. After just one over-the-counter dose of Benadryl my blood pressure lowered to dangerous levels. Against the professional opinions of all my doctors, I refused to use inhalers or become dependent on pharmaceuticals to keep my lungs open.

"Why would I teach my body to depend on drugs rather than build up their own function? Why would I subject myself to unbearable side effects when I saw a simple and very common sense solution? I chose to avoid cats and build up my immune system. Based on my refusal for medication, three doctors fired me as their patient."

For totally different reasons, Eddie understood what being "fired" from a doctor felt like. "I went through the entire list of doctors in my health insurance network. You know, that big huge book of providers? Not one of them would treat me because I'm Trans. And I don't even have anything really 'wrong' with me. I just want preventative care. But take me back to the operative phrase. You said you *used to* be allergic. What happened?"

"Later in my 20s, my parents found this intensive alternative therapy treatment, Nambudriped Allergy Elimination Technique (NAET). Twelve weeks and $1200 later, I was cured. I still have no idea how or why it worked. After my last treatment, I visited the Animal Humane Society and spent an hour playing with kittens without the slightest of symptoms. It was a miracle."

"Well, I choose to believe in miracles. So let's stick with your operative phrase. You USED TO BE allergic to cats. Not anymore." Eddie smothered the last coals with the same finality in his voice that affirmed the death of my allergies. We went inside. He assured me that his cats aren't allowed in the guest bedroom and told me to have sweet dreams.

I slept cat-allergy free, and more importantly, tear-free.

The next night, Eddie and I sat on the couch while he told me the story of his transition. The long-haired sickly ginger cat named "The Face" nestled onto Eddie's chest as if to comfort him through the darker parts of the story. Eddie openly answered all my ignorant questions, recognizing my curiosity as a desire to be educated.

When he talked about his choice to have a double mastectomy, he lifted up his shirt to show me how his surgeon carefully salvaged his nipples. The Face rubbed his cheek into Eddie's chest, and I watched the two of them savor a moment of silent surrender. There was this subtle energy of Protection coming off of The Face. He wanted to Protect Eddie from further pain, and he softened what he could with with furry and insistent snuggles.

A deeper layer of Protection hovered around Eddie as he shared with me his choice to forego a hysterectomy because of the health risks involved and the potential of significant loss in sexual pleasure. The deeper he got into his feelings around his choices, the bigger the Protection around him built, and the more attentive The Face became. Why subject himself to a more invasive and risky surgery while also compromising sexual sensation just to have a fake penis that wasn't likely to work properly?

Eddie explained to me that because he identified as a male, took male hormones, but had retained his female reproductive organs, he couldn't find a doctor to administer simple medical care such as an annual pap smear and pelvic exam. He told me again that he had personally called every single physician and medical provider in his health insurance network, and every one of them refused to provide him care.

"The day I called the last doctor in the book I learned a big lesson. No one, absolutely no one is going to advocate for me or Protect my rights and interests as well as I can for myself."

The Face, offended, batted Eddie across the cheek.

"Yes Face, I know, you will ALWAYS protect me."

Eddie's story reminded me of what I felt like as a meek 23-year-old woman having to stand up to older wiser physicians to Protect my choices to live a drug-free life. And just as I made that connection, The Face put his paw on my leg. Sitting between us on the couch, wearing the costume of a long-haired ginger cat, Protection (aka "The Face") put the first set of stitches into my wounds.

In leaving Ted, I made another unconventional life choice. I chose to go on the road and be "home-less" instead of getting a "real job" and settling into my own apartment. Like Eddie, my choice was mine alone, but one that caused some people to look at me sideways or challenge my decisions through passive aggressive questioning. As our conversation continued into the depths of mutual understanding about unconventional life choices, Protection, aka The Face, snuggled both of us. His chin and cheeks nuzzled for scratches from Eddie while his tail occasionally flicked and patted my leg.

"How did you sleep?" Eddie asked at the breakfast table.

"To be honest, I haven't slept well since Fuck You Sunday."

Chicken, the petite calico jumped onto the kitchen table and sat down next to my plate as if to say, "you're not alone."

"Chicken isn't exactly the most social of my kitties. She's rather aloof, so you should be honored that she is blessing you just now."

"Aw, thanks Chicken. I like you too." I said while giving her ear a scratch with the tip of my longest fingernail.

"She's picked you as one of her peeps. You're in a very elite club."

"Thanks Chicken. I'm honored."

"So, what's up with your sleep?" Eddie asked.

"I guess I haven't yet adapted to sleeping alone. It just feels so, well, alone." I said, and Chicken laid down on the table placing her paws perfectly next to each other just to the left of my plate. She looked me right in the eyes as if to say again, "you are NOT alone."

"After my surgery, my girlfriend broke up with me, and I had the same issue. I felt so cold, everything was so different that I couldn't find a way to be cozy," Eddie said as Chicken started cleaning her paws.

"I built this fortress of pillows around me, trying to simulate the sensation of another body in the bed with me. It didn't really work, until one day I woke up realizing I had slept through the whole night."

"What happened? What was different?"

"I woke up and realized I had fallen asleep spooning one of the pillows. But, the magic wasn't in the pillow. The magic was that I had slept the entire night holding my own hand. There was something so precious in that. I was loving myself, comforting myself. That day I realized the difference between Loneliness and Solitude. And I discovered the power of self-soothing."

Chicken jumped off the table and retreated to her solitary perch in the window.

"See," Eddie motioned to Chicken in her happy place. "Solitude."

I wanted to learn how to have that for myself. Outside Chicken's window, I saw Solitude waving to me, letting me know that she was there for me whenever I was ready. All I had to do was just open the window. Was this adventure of mine really a way to find how I could be myself fully? To figure out how to be Me without a partner beside me?

I admitted to myself, and out loud to Eddie, that maybe one day my new normal of divorce could teach me how to hold hands with Solitude.

That night, I piled up the pillows beside me as Eddie had suggested. In the morning I woke up with my arms wrapped around myself in a full embrace, my fingers interlacing with my ribs. I slept through the whole night. The first thing I did after getting out of bed was find Chicken in her window perch and pat her on the head.

"Thank you Chicken, for showing me that there is a difference between Loneliness and Solitude."

Solitude tapped on the glass of the window with a suture needle. I nodded acknowledgement and gratitude to her, for she had just stitched up a chunk of my wounds.

Each evening, after a long day of teaching workshops and trainings, I greeted Eddie with a happy "honey, I'm home," and the four cats would circle around us as we ate the meal Eddie had prepared from a new vegan recipe. Each meal was a family affair. Eddie had made the decision to go vegan just days before I arrived. Watching him transition from carnivore to vegan was refreshing and exciting for me. In some ways, just a few vegan meals with Eddie served as medicine to heal nearly 10 years of angry anorexic vegan meals with Ted.

In efforts to acquiesce Ted's eating disorder issues during my marriage, I explored various alternative nutrition and dietary lifestyles, including veganism. We had dabbled in meat-free, gluten-free, dairy-free, sugar-free, and many other "something-free" diets. For six months we even tried all-out RAW. For Ted, food was the greatest enemy.

For me, food was sacred. It was more than just a source of energy. I grew up in a house where we intentionally and purposefully ate meals together. It wasn't about my relationship with food—food, for me, *was* Relationship. As a result, eating and mealtimes triggered more arguments than anything else in my marriage. I loved cooking, which meant making a big mess in the kitchen. Ted's OCD caused him to clean up after me while I was still cooking, sometimes washing dishes I was still using.

I was raised to treat food with deep respect, and to always sit down at the table to eat, putting everything on a plate, even take-out.

The Gift Inside the Wound

Ted preferred to eat standing at the counter straight out of the container with the fridge door still open.

Eating roasted brussel sprouts one evening while Eddie's "velcro kitty," Captain Fluffy Pants circled between our legs begging for a dropping like a dog, I told Eddie about the tumultuous mealtimes with Ted. Between mouthfuls of perfectly roasted sprouts, I gushed with gratitude over the care and tenderness Eddie put into our meals together. A simple thank you turned into a monologue about how during my marriage I allowed Ted's eating disorder demon control our mealtimes. I ranted about how I gave up foods I loved for him, and how I grew to hate cooking. My monologue to Eddie ended with an exclamation about how excited I was to have my own kitchen again, to cook my way, what I wanted.

"Do you realize what you just did there?" Eddie finally interrupted. "You said you're looking forward to living alone. To be loyal to yourself first!"

(In my mind, the words "Loyal to Yourself" hovered over our heads like a meme....)

He went on. "Living alone," Eddie said as Captain Fluffy Pants pawed at his leg, again, like a dog, asking for a treat, "I have been afforded the opportunity to fall completely head over heels in love with myself."

"And my cats show me every day how to love myself. It's like the love they show me is simply a reflection of the potential love I have for myself. Especially this guy, my food-motivated-dog-in-a-cat-suit-dopey-sweet-goober boy." Eddie petted Captain Fluffy Pants head under the table, and Captain Fluffy Pants responded in complete Loyalty with a nose nudge and strut against his leg.

Eddie was right. I thought of Sukha. She was a reflection of how much I could and should love myself. Her kind soft brown eyes and warm snuggles were expressions of Loyalty. I wondered, why had I offered all my Loyalty to Ted? Why did I give him my soft brown eyes and warm snuggles when he didn't even appreciate them? Why wasn't I giving myself that Loyalty? Why didn't I bat my soft brown eyes at myself? Why not give myself warm snuggles?

Just as these questions popped into being, I heard Solitude knock from outside Chicken's window. I wanted to invite her in, but instead, Loneliness blew a cold wind over my quinoa. I couldn't fully ingest the newness of Loyalty just yet.

"Can I learn to be okay alone?" I asked, chewing on the tine of my fork.

"Most definitely," Eddie said. "But you can't know that until you try it. You're gonna have to just trust me on this one."

It felt like trusting my NAET therapist when I went to the Animal Humane Society after my last session.

"Will I ever not feel lonely?" I asked as Grief put that ugly frog back in my throat. I thought I might spit the brussel sprout across the table with a violent sob. I didn't know if I could swallow.

"Loneliness will always be there." Eddie answered, "But, isn't loneliness with yourself better than being lonely in a relationship?"

Eddie had a point there. I'd tried the loneliness in a relationship, and that sucked. It really sucked. If I were perfectly honest, in that moment at dinner with Eddie, talking about Loneliness, I was the farthest from lonely than I had been in years. And, I was able to swallow.

"What do I do with myself?" I asked, naively.

"That's easy. Whatever makes you happy. Do that."

Do that.

Do that.

Do that. Do that. Do that. Do that.

Those few words bounced around the room like a super ball. Eddie made it sound simple, to just boing boing boing from place to place and find joy in each space.

I spewed a half-eaten brussel sprout across the room. but not from an uncontrollable sob. Rather, I erupted in laughter. Another stitch wrapped its way through my wounds.

Captain Fluffy Pants scarfed it down instantly.

He looked up at me with gratitude and accomplishment, and licked his paw as if to say that he was rather proud of how he tied off his sutures.

My last night at Eddie's, while he went on his evening run, I took a few minutes with each of the cats to thank them for introducing me to new members of my Spirit Healing Team. I sat on the couch, and The Face nuzzled his face into my belly where the fingers of Protection stitched up my vulnerable holes from the inside. I greeted Chicken at her perch where she put her nose on the window that separated her whiskers from tickling Solitude's finger.

The Gift Inside the Wound

"When I figure out how to invite Solitude into my life, " I told Chicken, "I will remember it was you who introduced me to her."

I unhooked the bungee cord on the kitchen cabinet and watched as Captain Fluffy Pants helped himself to the kitty treat of his choice, and I thanked him for teaching me about Loyalty to myself.

Whatever makes you happy. Do that.

But…what do I want?

Lastly, I crawled down on the floor and gazed into the deep mysterious eyes of Eddie's black cat, Arch-Nemesis.

"Can you help me figure out the mystery of what makes me happy?" I asked her.

How ironic that the Mystery of my greatest happiness was revealed to me through the eyes of a cat named Arch-Nemesis.

Teri Leigh

Empowerment of the Red Queen

"There is nothing more attractive than an woman who carries herself like a Queen and wears her confidence like a crown!"
~Khari Toure'

After five days working in Tampa and staying with Eddie and his cats, I went to stay with my friend Olivia, Eddie's sister, for a mini-vacation. Eddie and his cats led me to the top of the rabbit hole of healing by forcing me to question my heart's desire. While I traveled down the rabbit hole, Eddie, a Queen in his own right, passed the healing scepter to his sister.

Olivia greeted me at the bottom of the rabbit hole wearing thigh high, spike-heel leather boots and a sexy red dress. The Red Queen, possessing the power to move in every direction in this game board of life, showed me a tiny door to a beautiful garden where She gets whatever Her heart desires.

"You'll be sharing a room with Christmas and Halloween," Olivia laughed as she showed me into her guest bedroom, overrun with holiday decorations and the visions of every child's heart's desires living inside unopened gifts and jack-o-lanterns filled with candy.

"The birth of the Christ and the honoring of the dead, I think I can handle that dichotomy," I replied. The ornaments seemed to fit with the death of my marriage juxtaposed with the birth of my Self.

Placing my suitcase on the floor between snowmen and witches, I noticed a mysterious black plush toy cat peering at me from the top shelf of the bookcase. She looked just like Eddie's black cat, Arch Nemesis. Being a queen (an un-neutered female cat) perhaps she could help me unlock the mysterious tiny door to my heart's desire. I moved her to the nightstand, inviting her to be my familiar. Little did I know, Arch Nemesis would haunt my dreams as well.

After showering off my travels, I met Olivia on her back deck for a late lunch. She had a beautiful plate of meats, cheeses, olives and berries with a bottle of fine red wine, the perfect start to an evening with my girlfriend.

"I feel like a queen here," I said, raising my glass.

"That's because you are one." Our glasses clinked. I could see her smile behind her sip.

"Darlin," she said, leaning forward a little. "I'm gonna show you just how to be a Queen."

"Promise?" I asked hesitantly, feeling like a tiny pawn stepping onto the chess board of life, wondering how I might ever make it across the eight giant squares to Queendom.

Olivia is a very special kind of friend. While I don't see her often and we can go months without communicating, just one look and we know exactly what's going on with each other on the inside.

The day after Fuck You Sunday, she messaged me, "Just to say hi, and I'm thinking of you," when we hadn't spoken in months.

She knew, without knowing.

The last time I saw Olivia, she was battling some pretty nasty demons as she was trudging her way through her own divorce process. At that time, she was just beginning to make friends with lots of powers of her own. She recognized (and perhaps Eddie had told her) that I was just starting to engage with my own Spirit Team in a new way.

When I landed on her doorstep, I saw Olivia stand with grace, as a Queen who reigned confidently over her domain. Having recently lost my own domain, I looked to her as a mentor who could guide me through the eight squares to my own Queening. She was prepared to educate me on the finer points of discovering and demanding my own heart's desires as a Queen.

My Fuck You Sunday wounds, now properly stitched, were just starting to heal and Olivia, The Red Queen who knows without knowing, offered me a sweet salve. She invited me to join her for an afternoon at the spa. Although I had often prescribed spa services, particularly pedicures, to my clients as a form of self-care, I had always had a hard time spending the money on such services for myself. It felt like I was trying to pretend to be something I wasn't, to adorn myself as shiny and bright in a fake way.

"Lesson number one in finding your heart after the devastation of divorce," Olivia said. "When someone offers you something, a gift, a compliment, a meal, or in this case, a day at the spa…say yes, thank you."

"Yes, thank you," I complied. I figured a trip to a high-end spa was medicine I needed to learn how to swallow.

"Girlfriend, tonight, I'm going to show you that every woman's body is her temple. And the Temple needs special care as well," she winked.

Olivia had the aura of a goddess who holds the key to mysteries of the unconscious, the woman who knows the secrets to the divine feminine. She was the Red Queen, not in a dripping-wealth-ruling-a-kingdom sort of way, but rather in the essence of embracing the femininity and motherhood.

She showed me that the spa is a laboratory for women to explore the secret garden of femininity, revealing the natural essence of themselves. I suppose that is why the best spa treatments are the ones that draw upon the most natural elements, like a mud bath or herbal bath with essential oils from flower essences.

After our spa treatments, we sat on her deck, once again, with a plate of cheese and fruit and sipping a new bottle of red wine.

"Have you met Empowerment yet?" She asked, and I almost choked on my wine. I hadn't told anyone, not even Eddie, about how I personified my Spirit Team. It was something I was writing in my journal, and hadn't shared with anyone. But, as she always does, Olivia just KNEW.

"No. I think I'm still trying to warm myself from the cold grip of Grief." I swallowed, and felt the familiar pressure on my throat again. "Will this lump in my throat ever stop? When will I have a day when I don't cry?"

"Yeah," she agreed. "That part sucks, but it gets better. I promise."

"Can you give me some hints to how to make it better faster?"

"Absolutely! The first thing I suggest you do is dust off those bare yogi feet of yours and put on a pair of heels."

I could count the times I wore heels on one hand. "Heels? Seriously? Sounds painful."

"Nah, not if you get the right fit."

She looked intently at me. Behind her smile was a serious look. "Heels make a woman feel powerful, and right now, you need to feel powerful." She went on the describe the different kinds of heels, from the classic pump to knee-high boots to a chunky Mary Jane.

Then, she launched into a monologue about the power of her favorite thigh-high spike-heel boots…in the bedroom.

"I'm nearly six feet tall as it is. And when I put on those boots and stand over the edge of the bed, the look he gives me makes me feel 12-feet tall, or taller. I am the QUEEN. My dear Sister, you don't yet know, but will soon find out, the best sex of your life comes AFTER divorce."

Wait…WHAT?

"Girlfriend, that 'mommy porn' trilogy trash that every suburban housewife is downloading to her e-reader to tickle her g-spot has nothing on me."

"Have you read it?" I asked.

"Hell no! Why would I when I've got the real thing in my bedroom every other weekend?"

"Do you mean to tell me that you are involved in an S&M relationship?" I was intrigued.

She smiled and took a big sip of her wine. The sparkle in her eyes matched that of one of the witches in my bedroom. My girlfriend was sharing a precious secret with me. She was a dominatrix!

"Let me be clear," she continued, "What my partner and I share is NOT S&M. Our relationship is a deeply spiritual dominant/submissive relationship. There's a distinct difference. Pop culture glamorizes the lifestyle…" she began, then paused. She was choosing her words carefully. "practice has nothing to do with pain or degradation of any kind. The basis of my partnership is rooted completely in honoring—and worshipping—feminine power.

Many of my clients referenced that trilogy of sexy novels in their sessions with me, so I read them to get a better understanding of what my clients were seeking. Frankly, I found them as boring as, well, drab shades of grey. To me they poorly depicted romance as attachment and neediness. The world of whips and gags and causing pain to create pleasure didn't interest me, but Olivia's story did.

"While I'm the dominant in the relationship, he, as the submissive is the one in control of every circumstance. We role play, and wear costumes, but it is not about me asserting power OVER him. Rather, he demands that I OWN my power. He worships and adores me, and if I show him my confidence, my strength, my strong sense of self, he rewards me with more adoration and worship."

"He was so high up in his career that he spent most of his life telling people what he wanted, and they'd do it for him. He knows how to claim a status, to own a position, so now he's showing me. But he's not showing me how to be powerful in a masculine sort of way, but he's honoring my feminine."

"How does he do that?" I asked with intense curiosity.

"When he was a teenager, he had an experience with a woman, a sort of Mrs. Robinson situation. I don't know any details, but it was significant for him. She left an indelible imprint on him. The result is that he recognizes the necessity of the feminine and honors the power of Woman."

"Can you give me an example?" I ate her story with every bite of brie and raspberry jam, licking my lips at every flavor.

"Sometimes, he spends thirty minutes worshipping my feet, and he won't stop until I tell him to. He doesn't just kiss and massage my feet, it's like he takes the entire thirty minutes to express to me, through his touch, just how beautiful and amazing and powerful and fabulous I am. He talks to my feet, whispers sweet nothings to them, and fully appreciates every corner between every toe, acknowledging every crevice and line and curve and arch of each foot. It's like he is honoring every miniscule part of my being."

"That sounds delicious."

"Oh sister…It is delicious!"

"Except I don't know how I would be comfortable with that. I'd get shy."

"At first it was really uncomfortable, awkward even," she said. "Then he got me the thigh-high spike-heel boots. I tell you, they did something to me. They helped me to relax into the power, to surrender to the strength."

I rubbed my own feet, callused from years of walking yoga room floors. They'd only worn hiking shoes and comfy clogs for the last several years. I didn't know if they would tolerate any kind of heel.

"The spike heels help, AND, you might also consider a trip to the lingerie store," she winked.

I gulped again. My lingerie consisted mostly of sports bras and yoga tops. She was right. If I wanted to make my way across the board and own the Queen's power of moving in every direction, I needed to dress the part and own the power. Zip-up hoodies wouldn't pass as a Queen's robe.

"In the bedroom, and really anytime I am with him, I get anything and everything I want. It's like that 1980s movie, *The Princess Bride*, where Princess Buttercup asks the farm boy to do menial tasks for her and he complies with a simple 'as you wish.'

Not because he's her slave, but because she deserves it. The hard part for me, at first, was figuring out what I wanted. That took time. As a woman, especially as a mother, I have always put the needs and desires of others before myself."

"Yeah, I don't have any clue what I want, much less how to ask for it," As I said that, I could've sworn I heard the screech of a cat from across the back yard. Arch Nemesis?

"He challenges me," she continued, "to think about what it is in my life that I always wanted and never got. We'd have long conversations about dreams and fantasies, and then he'd invite me to play those scenarios out into sexual role plays. It's like I get to play in a new playground every time I see him.

"I will never run out of things I want, and he will never tire of providing me with my heart's desire. Given that we only see each other every other weekend, when Tori is with her dad, I have time in between our trysts to contemplate what I might want."

"I cannot imagine that," I admitted. "I always want to put others before myself, and I suppose it's so easy to think I wouldn't deserve it."

She nodded. "The thing is, he shows me that I deserve it, and that the bedroom is MY domain, the place where I get to put myself first. He puts me first. He empowers and affirms me, not through kinky sex tricks but through the energy of reverence and adoration. He submits to me, surrenders completely and shows me the greatness that I am."

"What's that feel like?" I started sipping on a second glass of wine.

"I know it sounds cheesy, but the only word to describe it is empowering. You know what I've noticed? Since I met him, I feel like I've grown a couple inches. I walk taller, and I look people more in the eye. It's changed everything about my world, absolutely everything!"

"Really?" I was envious. She had found a magic drug, and I wanted to try a dose.

"It hasn't been easy. There are rules. A big learning curve."

"Rules?"

"Yes. He will not give me anything unless I specifically ask for it, and he never denies me anything I request. I have to be very clear. That's why I say that he is the one in control. He taught me how to figure out what I want, and how to ask for it. TeriLeigh, it's so empowering! In the bedroom, I get to play with what *I* want. He treats me like a queen because I claim it. I own it."

"Can you give me an example?" I asked.

As if on cue, Olivia's 10-year-old daughter Tori came out from her bedroom and asked for dinner.

"Mommy, I want miso soup."

"As you wish," Olivia winked at me. "We can go to your favorite sushi place."

"Yes, Please." Tori said, "Did you read my speech for school?"

"Yes, Tori, I did." Olivia affirmed, but she refused to offer any comment or feedback on the speech because Tori didn't ask for it.

"What did you think?"

"I thought it was beautiful, like you are. The message was so full of love, like you are."

I heard the tone of reverence and honoring in Olivia's voice. In this case, Olivia took on the role of submissive to Tori. She honored and adored Tori, and only gave her exactly what she requested. Tori didn't ask for criticism, she asked only for an opinion. As a submissive, Olivia was obligated to offer only reverence, unless Tori asked for something different.

"Was there anything you think I should improve?" Tori asked for the criticism.

"I noticed there were a few spelling mistakes of words that I know that you know how to spell." Olivia offered suggestions for improvement, heavily coated in sweetness and adoration.

"Was there anything else I can do better?" Tori asked for more.

"I also noticed that it didn't look like your best handwriting, because I know what you are capable of doing. I think it is great, and you can turn it in like it is, or you can choose to fix the spelling errors and re-write it in your best handwriting."

"I can do that," Tori said.

"It's your choice," Olivia reminded Tori of her power. "It's not due until Monday right?"

"I don't want to re-do it now. Can we go to sushi now?"

"As you wish. Sushi it is," Olivia said, "You have all weekend to decide if you want to re-do it or not. The choice is yours."

In that tiny exchange about Tori's speech, Olivia offered Tori the affirmation that she is beautiful and that she produces good work. Yet, she empowered Tori to make her own decision about whether she wanted to turn in the work as is or to revise it to be a better reflection of Tori's ability. In many ways, in the small exchange, I witnessed Olivia step into the submissive role, providing the lessons of empowerment to her daughter as the dominant.

Tori scampered back to her bedroom to get her shoes as Olivia gathered up the plates and empty wine glasses, refusing to let me help.

"TeriLeigh, do you know how blessed I am to have this amazing child in my life? Learning the dominant/submissive relationship has changed my parenting for the better.

I am so different with her. I get to channel this power I feel directly into her. She accepts it! She doesn't need to be taught how to own it. It's like she is this adorable little mirror that shows me what it means to be a woman. I only get to be with my man every other weekend, but she is here with me every single day. I get to honor her like he honors me."

The Panther's Desire

*"Desire is the starting point of all achievement,
not a hope, not a wish,
but a keen pulsating desire which transcends everything."*
~Napoleon Hill

When I crawled into bed that night, Grief clutched my throat once again, and I cried. I couldn't tell if my wails were my own or the cackles of the witches of the Halloween decorations strewn about the room. Arch Nemesis the black cat I'd moved to the night stand taunted me, and the snowmen chilled me. I spun between holidays and bounced between seasons, and all the commotion was like a tilt-a-whirl in my stomach.

Could the bed spins be from bad sushi and too much wine? But, three glasses of wine over the course of four hours wasn't enough to make me drunk. If it was bad sushi, Olivia and Tori should've been ill as well. Whatever it was, my stomach churned as if something wanted out. And I ran to the adjoining bathroom, and wretched.

I hadn't thrown up like this in years. My stomach's contents felt like they were forcibly ejected from my guts. It felt like two giant hands reached down my throat and scoured my insides, scraping the walls of my stomach and intestines with long talon-like fingernails, scratching out of the corners and cracks all the crap I had swallowed over the years. In violent heaves, all the lies I thought about myself, all the insults I ingested came pouring out.

The stuff I threw up came from far beyond the recent wounds of my marriage. The hands probed inside my core and ripped out a thicket of insecurities that grew from seeds from back in my childhood , from the time I was Tori's age, and before. It dug into memories of childhood bullying, adolescent conditioning, and college insecurities. I felt as though I was flushing out the weight of pains of every trauma that squeezed and squelched my sense of self.

"Are you okay, sweetie? Would you like some water?" Olivia came to check on me. I recognized the tone in her voice, deliberately putting me into the dominant role. I remembered Tori's simple reply.

"Yes, thank you."

By the time she brought me a glass of water, I had finished my last heave, completely wrung out and raw from the inside out. She handed me the glass, and I sipped it like it was medicine. It smoothed the rough edges that had been scraped by the thorny brambles I had ejected from my system.

"Thank you. I feel much better."

"Can I get you anything else?"

"No, thank you." I was too raw, scathed and beaten by the regurgitation of past injustices. I couldn't figure out what else I might want, at least not just now.

"You let me know if and when you want anything. I'll be right upstairs."

"I will. Thank you." When I crawled into bed, I was a bit delirious from the effects of my spontaneous detoxification. While the bed spins had subsided, I started to feel subtle hallucinations. While I lay there somewhere between asleep and awake, I watched as the various characters of Christmas and Halloween came alive in my imagination.

Mother Mary was conspiring with the witches to take control of my dreams as the snowmen and ghosts stood at attention like soldiers waiting for orders from their queen.

When I finally surrendered to full slumber, I was welcomed into a vivid dream that seemed more real than imaginary.

I was walking along the beach, the Florida ocean waters threatening to lap at my feet with every step, but I stepped away from the water with every wave. Until one rushing wave came rushing up and I couldn't escape. As soon as the wave swallowed my foot, my entire body was sucked into the ocean. The next thing I knew, I was in a mountain forest, my feet submerged in a rocky stream.

This had to be a dream, or was it?

Day shifted to night as quickly as my foot had been pulled underwater, and the echo of crickets sounded vaguely like the cackle of the witches in Olivia's guest bedroom. My eyes adjusted quickly, and I felt more natural in the woods than I ever had before, like I had shape-shifted from human-being into a creature of the night.

I knew I was being watched, but not by an owl in a neighboring tree or a raccoon hunting for his evening meal. The eyes I felt were more penetrating, like a predator trying to decide if I was worthy prey. Yet my defenses weren't raised. I had this un-nerving calm inside me, like the wild animal who has lived a long full life and was ready to surrender to the fate of death.

And then I saw him, a black panther. His piercing blue eyes caught just the tiniest glimmer of the new moon. I hadn't a moment to take a breath because as soon as I saw him, he pounced. I was flat on my back, the soft earth underneath me, his paw pinned to my heart. His claws pierced my clothing and barely touched the skin of my chest. I felt both the pressure of his weight on me with a simultaneous lifting sensation, like his claw was a vacuum pulling at my heart, which now pulsated outside of my ribcage.

I was not this panther's prey; I was his mate.

I relished the pressure of his body pushing me deeper into the earth, like he was trying to show me how to merge with the Mother, to remind me of the womb from which I came at the same time as introducing me to the womb inside me. I wanted more weight.

I wanted his density on every exposed part of my body to push me deeper into the soil. I wanted the cracks and crevices that had been emptied from my sickness to be filled with the fullness of earth and soil below me as well as the wildness and ferocity of the beast on top of me.

Within the soil, my pores could ingest the medicine of femininity. The mud coated every hair follicle and penetrated my skin. From the panther, I could inhale the medicine of masculinity. His heavy hot breath permeated my lungs, and I felt like he was showing me how to reclaim the savage being inside me.

The heaviness and density of his weight on my body was directly proportionate to the vacuum suction of his claw on my heart. The more of me that connected with Mother Earth, the fuller my heart felt, and the stronger it beat in my body, emitting multiple ejaculations of hormonal power into my bloodstream.

The panther lapped at my face with his sandpaper tongue. With each stroke, he purred. The vibrations of his vocal chords coupled with the roughness of his tongue stirred up the sediment on my skin for him to lick away. While my sickness had expelled toxins from my insides, the panther lapped away the toxins from my outsides.

My vision, my hearing, my sense of smell all heightened. His teeth got tangled in my hair, with each tug of my scalp, I felt as though the strands of my hair became more like antennae—the longer they grew, the more my intuition and receptivity were enhanced.

When my face and neck were clean, yet not quite raw, he allowed me to sit up. He pushed his chin into my shoulder and strutted the length of his body against my arm and back, right down to the end of his tail. I leaned into him as a cat does when she wants to be petted, and he reciprocated. We strutted around each other like this, his fur lapping at my skin like a brush, soothing the subtle itches and irritations and massaging the muscles and tissues in each other, calming and nurturing each other to an utter state of bliss.

Finally, we wrapped around each other, like a cat with her kitten. I was both fully satiated and at the same time, voraciously hungry. My body was completely exhausted, yet my mind felt energized, fully awake. In the place between sleep and awake, I could still feel my panther's paw on my chest, tugging at my soul like the aftershocks of orgasm. I became keenly aware of the ghosts and snowmen surrounding me, silenced. But Arch Nemesis, on the night-table next to me, she spoke, in Eddie's voice.

Whatever you want. Do that.
Do that.
Do that.

My panther wanted to show me my deepest desires.
I needed to pay attention.

I entered a meditative state, my mind traced every tiny buzzing left lingering in my body from the dream, alert and curious to make meaning of the sensations. Little tiny blue lightning bolts extended from each claw and sent electric shocks into my heart, awakening

The Gift Inside the Wound

cells and particles inside me, reminding me of dreams and fantasies I had developed in my childhood.

Each shock stimulated a nerve pathway from my heart through various parts of my body, and I felt the referred sensations right down to my fingertips, the backside of my naval, the underside of my kneecaps, the insides of my thighs, and the bottoms of my earlobes. If I traced each nerve pathway sensation from its root in my heart to its tip, I could discover the messages it carried to me about my deepest dreams and desires and fantasies and ideals.

The panther's claw that rested at the very base bottom tip of my heart touched the nerve that extended down to the tips of my fingers. The squeeze of the panther's claw rolled heavy metal pinballs into the tips of my fingers, reminding me of the sensation of punching the heavy metal keys of my mother's old manual typewriter when I was a child. I loved the feeling of my fingers pushing into the key and how the key moved the levers under the key that made the letter strike the paper over and over, again and again—until the letters formed words, and the words formed sentences, and the sentences formed ideas.

The force of my fingers on the keys made something as simple as ink and paper into whole worlds, different realities. I'd discovered at that young age that if I didn't punch the keys hard enough, the ink didn't penetrate the paper as deep and the word carried a softer flavor while if I struck the key with passion, a denser emotion, it tattooed the paper with a heavier intensity. While writing my stories, in grade school, middle school, and even high school, I played with the pressure on the page and consciously chose which words to emphasize with either softness or hardness, with smoother curves or sharper edges.

In college, instead of pressure on the typewriter keys, I used colored pencils to highlight the different letters and sounds in the poetry books of Langston Hughes and Dylan Thomas and Maya Angelou.

Like the pressure of my panther's claw on my heart, and the pressure of my pinball heavy fingers on the typewriter keys, I wanted my words to penetrate the irises of my readers. That maybe, just maybe, the energy inside the pulse of my heart could enter their bloodstreams and make them feel, REALLY FEEL.

I want to WRITE!

The claw of the panther that reached around the left side of my heart and encircled the whole left side and sent an oozing warm liquid through the twisty and windy nerve pathway that slithered through my vital organs. This warm fluid navigated its way through the mess of my intestines, flushing through my ovaries and uterus, ending with an effervescent bubbling at the inside folds of my naval.

The warmth reminded me of the sensation of drinking mom's homemade hot chocolate or warm soup after a long day of sledding or ice skating, like being warmed from the cold on the inside. And, tt reminded me of the feeling I would get when my dad would open his winter coat and zip me up inside it with him while standing outside in a Minnesota chill. Every once in a while, the oozing liquid would emit a tiny twinge, a surge of pulsation, a kind of butterfly-in-the-stomach jump that I would get from a new romance. This feeling was of being loved.

I wanted to be held, nurtured, loved, caressed, touched, and completely enveloped by love!

Another of the panther's claws touched the front side of my heart and sent a similar oozing liquid through the marrow of my bones into the tender space behind my kneecaps.

It reminded me of the feeling of my grandmother's sponge cushion kneepads and how as a little girl I wanted my own pair so that I could kneel on the kitchen floor and clean out the corners under the cabinets where my little fingers could reach and hers couldn't. I didn't want to be like grandmother, or emulate her behavior. I just wanted to be helpful. I wanted to do something for her that she couldn't do for herself.

I want to serve and support others, to help them when they cannot help themselves.

On the other side, the right side of my heart, one of the panther's claws actually penetrated the outer wall of my heart, causing a tiny slit. Blood from this tiny wound spilled around the outside of my heart, and the subtle pain from the wound sent a cluster of stinging and piercing sensations through a nerve pathway down my spinal cord. Then, as if these sensations had a mind of their own, they shot down both legs, bounced off the bottoms of my heel bones and ricocheted up my thighs, causing a slight puckering sensation on the inside of each thigh.

The sum of these sensations were sharp and fast, and they moved in waves—and at times like a swarm. Their movement ignited excitement and wildness inside me. It reminded me of the feeling in my legs when I was finally old enough to jump off the high dive a the neighborhood swimming pool.

I was one of those children who ran faster than I could think when it came to facing my fears. When I got the idea to jump off the high dive, I scurried up the ladder as fast as I could and ran right off the plank, not giving myself time to stop and think about what I was doing, not letting fear have a moment to get in my way.

My whole life, like everyone, I have fears, but somehow, when I really want something, I blindfold myself to my fears. Instead, I give myself permission to run through those fears and bypass the process of weighing pros and cons. Along with this comes an excitement, a sense of urgency for adventure.

There is a side of me that believes life is about the adventure, trying out all the different ways this human body can have sensations. As long as I know something is safe, I want to try it. It was this part of me that didn't think about the consequences of packing my car for a destination unknown unplanned road trip without an end date. I just got in the car and drove off the deep end to see what might happen.

I want adventure!

While running in the direction of adventure, I felt the last of the panther's claws squeeze the part of my heart that sent sharp and fast sensation up the back of my neck where it boomeranged inside my skull, finally landing at the bottom tips of my earlobes, triggering various thoughts and ideas and concepts and insights in all parts of my brain.

Like a ping pong ball bouncing randomly through the sphere of my skull, the sensation didn't have any rhyme or reason to how it triggered thoughts in my head. As a little girl, I loved playing connect the dots, particularly those drawings that had the numbers zigzagging across the page in ways that didn't make sense until the whole picture was complete.

My favorite part of my college education wasn't any one particular class or even the depth of exploring my triple majors, but the interconnectedness of all of the classes. I was most excited when I could connect a lesson in my astronomy class to something in Latin poetry to something else in 20th century American history.

I want to feel and fully KNOW the interconnectedness EVERYTHING!

In that space between sleep and awake, the panther pawed at my chest, over and over. It was as if he were pulling my heart's desires right out of my chest. Powerless to his panting, I surrendered to his pawing. Every stroke, I replied as I had been trained by the Red Queen.

"Would you like to spend your life as a writer?"
"Yes, Thank you."
"Would you like to hold and be held by a compassionate partner?"
"Yes, Thank you."
"Would you like to serve and provide to other and be appreciated for the gifts you offer?"
"Yes, Thank you."
"Would you like a life of exploration and adventure?"
"Yes, Thank you."
"Would you like space in your every single day to contemplate the interconnectedness of everything?"
"Yes, Thank you."

Over coffee the next morning, I told Olivia about my dream and the panther. She smiled a knowing smile and said, "I know that dream. Mine was a lion."

The Gift Inside the Wound

Bandaging the Wound ~ Receiving Love

Teri Leigh

The Gift Inside the Wound

Yes, Thank You

*"The nourishment of the body is food,
while the nourishment of the soul is feeding others."*
~Imam Ali

Olivia taught me the power of "yes, thank you" and the panther and Arch Nemesis showed me what I really want out of life, yet I still felt empty. I knew what I wanted, what I needed even, but how do I get them to be reality in my world? I felt like the dreams and desires of my heart pierced by the claws of the panther were around the corner, out of reach, carrots on a perpetually moving stick.

The last seven weeks had left me feeling like the wind had been sucked from my lungs and the blood was drying from my heart. Even though blessings were showering over me like confetti in the wind, I felt like I couldn't catch enough of them to really matter. Like trying to catch snowflakes on my tongue to quench my thirst. While once in a while I'd catch one and squeal with glee for a moment or two, I still felt parched. Somehow, I was driving through the humid ocean air of Florida, yet my skin couldn't figure out how to open its pores to receive the moisture into my being.

Had I been cursed? Had Ted's Fuck Yous penetrated my being and made it so I was unable to receive the blessings and abundance offered to me?

I left Olivia's place on the Atlantic coast and drove across central Florida to Apollo Beach, a small canal town across the bay from Tampa where my friends Julie and Tim snow-birded from Minnesota with their two therapy dogs each winter. Nearly seven weeks after Fuck You Sunday, when I felt like my world had taken so many things from me, Julie held a mirror for me, reminding me of my own teachings.

Here, my dear friend, this is how to receive.

Julie was a retired science teacher and breast cancer survivor. Tim was a retired high school math teacher and a Vietnam Marine Corp Vet. Once upon a time I taught high school English one floor down from Tim's math classroom. When I traded my classic literature curriculum guides for yoga blocks and straps, Julie joined me 3-5 days a week as her retirement gift to herself. As a teacher, a mother, and a wife to a man enduring posttraumatic stress from Vietnam, Julie spent her life giving. She came to yoga to learn how to receive. Through yoga practice, I coached her through breast cancer and a mastectomy. Over the years, I had taught her to say "yes, thank you" and to welcome the gifts and abundance offered to her in gratitude for her generosity.

In my years of working one-on-one with clients, I have come across dozens of cases of breast cancer. Each and every one was a beautiful soul whose heart was too full of compassion to be contained. The word compassion is derived from the Latin meaning *to suffer together*. I had come to learn from these clients that breast cancer patients are women who have made a lifestyle of suffering with and for others. The breast is symbolic of mothering, unconditional nurturing provided by a mother. From the breast flows the milk of abundance, all-giving, the source ultimate source of every need. The common denominator in all my breast cancer clients was that they had suffered with and for so many people in their lives that they put their own needs on the backburner. In essence, they had been giving compassion too much for too long and needed to receive.

As Julie's yoga teacher, I taught her how to find a better balance with compassion. While Julie's life purpose was about compassion, serving others through their traumas and pains, she often gave more than she had to give, putting her own needs last. Her practice became a way to give to herself first, like the flight attendants say on the airplane, to put the mask on yourself first, and then assist others. Over the years I worked with her, I watched her establish better boundaries with those in need. I watched her determine clear priorities for herself. She not only learned poses and sequences, she absorbed the deeper esoteric wisdoms threaded into the practice. Julie was my greatest success story, my best testimonial, and my most dedicated student.

My goal as a teacher is always to teach myself out of a job. My hope is that I show my students how to pull out of themselves what they already know, eventually not needing me to hold the mirror to their light. On the day I closed my yoga studio, we shared an unspoken hug, knowing that she had graduated and didn't need me to guide her anymore. She had learned how to give to herself first, how to receive, and thus to give and receive in balance.

As all things always come full circle, now it was time for me, the teacher, to become the student, and for Julie, my student, to become my teacher.

When I pulled into Julie and Tim's driveway, my body was warm from the greenhouse effect of the Florida sun in my car, but my heart shivered. Although the chill of my Minnesota north woods Grief Ritual was several weeks in my rearview mirror, I still felt the bitter bite of Fuck You Sunday every day, afraid of the cold empty chill that might come at any moment. A simple thought, or smell, or a memory of Ted, would blast the freezer door open on my heart leaving a coating of frost all over my insides. I had yet to go a day without bone chills and tears streaking down my cheeks like icicles.

Julie opened the door and pulled me into an embrace. I felt like she was folding me into a heavy homemade quilt, the kind that was meticulously hand-stitched from the fabric scraps of favorite pieces of clothing. Wisps of her hair lapped at my face like the fringes of the quilt. When I tried to let go, she held on tight, pulled me in tighter even. She warmed me like homemade hot chocolate after a long day of ice skating on a frozen Minnesota lake. In less than two months, almost everything I held onto in my life had lost its grip. I'd watched my marriage and my home float away in the sky like helium balloons. I was losing my grip on my career as well, like a flower I had dropped into the river. I couldn't dive in and swim to get it, but I wasn't yet ready to turn and walk away from it either. I had gotten so used to things pulling out of my hands that being held onto by Julie was foreign.

For the first time in the seven years I had known Julie, I let her see me cry. She held me, and I wept. Time stopped as my water flowed. But this time, my tears were warm. Soothing even. They dripped from my chin, and she absorbed them in her second womb, the empty space between us where her left breast once was. I knew that for the next five days I had no choice but to receive love in every form Julie knew how to give. Starting first and foremost with that hug.

Yes, Thank you.

Our embrace was interrupted when the front door burst open as two black labs waggled their way to us on the lanai, followed by Julie's husband, Tim. Semper, the younger of the two, barreled into me until I fell to the ground in a gaggle of giggles. Her tail wagged with more force than her sleek body could handle. Her wiggles tickled me until my crying instantly shifted into laughter. She planted her paw firmly on my breastbone, faintly familiar of the panther's paw, her tongue licked the salty tears from my face. Millie, the older of the two, patiently waited her turn as I wrestled my way to momentary happiness under Semper's *always faithful* giddiness.

While Julie set herself to fixing lunch, Tim rescued me from Semper's slobber and greeted me with a hug. Then, he handed me over to the healing powers of Millie, the skilled therapy dog. I sat down at the table to wait for lunch with Millie's head resting on my thigh. The pressure of her head on my leg simultaneously comforted me and pushed more tears through my body and out my eyes.

"Today is Ted's birthday," I said, choking on the words in my throat. "Should I call him?"

"No!" Julie said as she put a plate of food in front of me. "And I'll give you three reasons why not. One, he doesn't celebrate birthdays anyway. Two, he would only make you sad. And three, I don't want you to. Now stop thinking about him – I won't even say his name. Now, EAT!"

Although plenty of people had served me glorious meals since Fuck You Sunday, I hadn't really had an appetite since sometime before Christmas. After seven weeks away from Ted and his eating disorder, eating still wasn't exactly an enjoyable experience for me.

But when Julie said EAT, I ate.
And boy did it taste good!

Of course, she served me BLTs, and bacon ALWAYS makes everything better. Julie's BLT wasn't an average bacon, lettuce, and tomato sandwich. She added fresh basil and avocado, and I think even a sprinkle of garlic salt and onion powder. She used heirloom homegrown or farmer's market tomatoes and special fresh bakery bread. She served me on a table on the lanai, with fresh cut flowers. And, she refused to let me talk about anything sad. Instead, she told me happy stories about volunteering at the manatee center, scrunching up her nose and changing her voice when she told me about her encounters with the teddy bears of the sea.

The first bite was nothing short of divine. The crisp bread crust and salty bacon coupled with the tangy sweetness of the juicy ripe tomato, flavors popped and exploded on my tongue and teeth and cheeks and throat. Each burst of flavor tickled something in my nervous system that triggered my tummy into tune. For the first time in months, I felt hunger. AND, food tasted better than good. While I was licking my fingers to sop up every last crumb of the sandwich, Julie set about to making me a second without even asking.

"This is SOOO yummy!" I said as she plopped the plate in front of me again, a fresh sandwich awaiting my devouring.

"That's because my BLTs are filled with lots of TLC!"

Julie's maiden name is Cook. Although she took Tim's name at marriage, she kept the Cook in her for every meal she prepared. One of her many talents is spilling the contents of her heart and love onto every dish she prepares. She serves every meal with just the right dose of hugs and kisses and happy giggles to nurture and nourish not just the body, but every corner of the human soul. I ate two and a half sandwiches and two-thirds of a plateful of her hand-cut spicy steak fries. I felt nourished, and nurtured, and complete.

Yes, Thank you.

Teri Leigh

The Gift Inside the Wound

The Labrador Lean

> *"I have found that when you are deeply troubled,
> there are things you get from the silent devoted companionship of a dog
> that you can get from no other source."*
> ~Doris Day

While Julie's bacon, lettuce, tomato, avocado, basil, tender, loving care sandwiches planted seeds in my belly to trigger my appetite, I was cold. My internal heater still wasn't working. Even though I had been in Florida for several weeks, away from the bitter winter cold of the upper Midwest, I felt chilled. All. The. Time. Whenever any part of my body touched something cold—toes on the cold tile floor, fingers on a tub of ice cream, nipples on the lukewarm swimming pool water—I felt like the cold leaked right through a fracture line to my heart. And I shivered. The shivers mimicked the rhythms of my sobbing, and triggered a response in my nervous system that turned on my water works. To stay warm, I wore a black uniform—long black yoga pants, a thick black hoodie with thumb holes, and black wool knee-high socks.

I had yet to go a day without crying since Fuck You Sunday. Were my tears pulling the heat out of my body with them? Each time I cried, which was still several times a day, the gaping gash left by the knife wounds of Fuck You between and underneath my shoulder blades flooded with cold damp air and a frost around my lungs and heart.

After licking my plate clean, I zipped up my black hoodie sweatshirt, pulled up my wool knee-high socks and the waistband of my thick black yoga pants and curled up on a chaise lounge on the lanai deck for an afternoon nap. Millie, Julie, and Tim's older black lab, a trained and certified therapy animal, circled herself into a ball at the crook of my knees. She bowed her head, resting it on top of my thigh, as if to say, "I know the rawness and vulnerable place you are in, and I bow to you."

Millie and I stayed still as statues for a long time. We were still enough that Mr. Blue Heron thought it was safe enough to land a few feet from us on the other side of the lanai screen.

My first thought was, "Ted loves herons. I should call him." And then I'd remember that picking up the phone to share tiny happy moments like this with him wasn't part of my world anymore.

So I wept.

But this time, my crying was different. I didn't feel the gash between my shoulders blades open. The cold bristle on my bones didn't prick me. I didn't shudder or shiver. Instead, the water just trickled, and what came out was a soft fountain flow, like warm honey stretching down my cheeks. While the tears weren't soothing, they didn't sting. The pain was—bearable? Somehow, Millie's Labrador lean absorbed the pain's sharpest shards.

I let Millie's weight put me to sleep, a much needed nap. I slept for over two hours, longer than I had slept in one stretch in weeks.

I awoke when Semper brought me the gift of Julie's worn and dirty gardening shoe. She dropped it smack on my chest, sat down and wagged her tail, which in turn wagged her whole body. For a tiny half of a moment, I ached at the thought that Ted discarded me like a worn out pair of shoes that no longer felt good on his feet. Millie smelled my half a breath of despair and readjusted herself, crawling her front legs up my torso, planting her chin just under the worn out gardening shoe. Semper smiled at me with pride, a drop of drool landed on her clumsy black paw. Their message came through very clear.

The worn out shoes are the most comfortable, the favorite, the BEST.

In my next breath, I laughed. I realized that for the first time since Fuck You Sunday, I awoke and didn't feel like I wanted to crawl back into slumber. Rather, I felt like I wanted to be awake because this moment, this puppy pleasure moment was a not a nightmare.

Yes, Thank you.

The Gift Inside the Wound

Laying on the chaise lounge on the lanai with Millie *lab*-leaning between my legs was where Millie and I spent most of our time while I was at Tim and Julie's those five days. Millie's comforting weight grounded me, and the sun's shower of orange-yellow warmth protected me from chills. The only interruptions to my dog-sun sessions were Julie's meals and Semper's slobbery waggles. The fracture lines that allowed cold to seep into my heart began to close.

Just that week, Tim received word that Millie had WON the *Animal Companion of the Year Award* by the Minnesota Veterinarian's Association. As I spent the week in her care, I became intimately familiar with the skills she had that earned her that accolade.

That's why Millie was my perfect support in that time. She didn't ever ask me what I needed, or ask me how she could help. She just gave what she had. Unconditionally. She laid next to me and put her head on my leg. She absorbed my tears, sopped up my pain, listened without interrupting, and heard me without talking. She didn't expect a single thing of me. She let me just be as I was.

Millie couldn't say to me "what can I do to help you?" She couldn't say "just call me if and when you need anything." She simply intuited what I needed, and she did just that and gave to me. She listened without interrupting, and she heard me without talking. She was a natural empath.

One of the things that frustrated me in talking to people about my situation was when they would ask me HOW they could help me. I was so shell-shocked and uprooted by everything, I couldn't answer that question. I didn't know what I needed, much less what to tell someone to do for me. My delegation skills were defunct. Besides, asking for help was foreign to me. I'd been taught, as a good Midwesterner of Norwegian descent to never ever be a burden on others.

Of course I needed help. Of course I needed support. And, I was getting better at saying 'yes, thank you' when someone offered me something. But, to expect me to ask for help AND state exactly what to do to help me, well, that responsibility was more than I could handle.

For the last several weeks I sat at many dinner tables with many people who loved me, and they asked me to tell them my story. I didn't like the broken record sound of my own voice retelling the Fuck You Sunday story and the history behind it. I sounded pathetic. Millie let me rummage through the stuff that lived in storage underneath the story. In her presence I could dust off old feelings. And I could tell her my story without even speaking in coherent sentences, or even in English. Instead, she heard and understood me through the language of sobs and incomprehensible utterances. She didn't hand me a tissue to wipe away my tears, and more often than not, she didn't even lick them away. She just let them fall. With Millie, I felt safe to let my waters flow.

Millie let me just be.

One morning towards the end of my stay, while Julie did yoga on the pool deck I received an email confirming that yet another potential yoga job had disintegrated. For months I had been working to finalize a contract with a studio I visited twice a year to lead a portion of their teacher training. It was my biggest contract, and my most consistent job. The studio had come up against hard financial times and wanted to renegotiate my pay. When their final offer came through at a price that had me paying more out of pocket for travel expenses than I would earn, I swallowed hard (but I didn't cry) and wrote a simple reply to the email, declining their last offer and hit send.

As I gulped and swallowed after hitting send, the familiar crying feeling began to creep up into my throat. At just that moment, Millie arose from her sleeping spot at the head of Julie's mat and lengthened into a deep down dog, as if bowing to Julie's warrior pose. Despite Julie's crooked toes and the slight knottiness in her somewhat arthritic fingers, the look in her eye was the epitome of a woman warrior. Her stance was solid, and her gaze was strong. She looked radiant. Then Millie turned a quarter-turn and lengthened into a full up-dog in my direction before stepping up onto the chaise lounge and gifting me with another *lab lean*.

She looked me straight in the eye before she lowered her chin onto my knee. Her voice spoke clearly to me: "You are a warrior too, and everything is gonna be all right."

Twenty minutes later, Julie sat up from her final resting pose of her practice and said, "Every once in a while I think I'm in charge, and then the bigger spirit lets me know that's not the plan. Then I feel better."

Yes, Thank you.

Now-ness and Power-Posing

"The past has no power over the present moment."
~Eckhart Tolle

As Julie rolled up her yoga mat, Tim had returned from his morning round of golf. Julie set to fixing breakfast while I scratched Millie's ear, and we all listened to Tim's excitement about his discovery on the green.

"My therapist at the VA recommended I read *The Power of Now* by Eckhart Tolle, and so I've been practicing 'now-ness' while I golf."

Julie winked at me with a knowing grin. Both of us had been encouraging Tim to try yoga and meditation and mindfulness for years. "How did you find 'now-ness' today honey?" She said, always happy to watch him tell stories.

"I saw this Ted Talk the other day about Power-Posing. That if you stand in a power pose and breathe for two minutes before doing a specific task, you will perform better." As he spoke, he bounced around the pool deck, unable to contain the excitement in his body. He looked like a little kid who couldn't wait for something to happen.

"Oh, TeriLeigh, you gotta watch this Ted Talk, by a social psychologist at Harvard Business School. She says that you shouldn't just 'fake it to make it' but you gotta 'fake it to become it.'" I made note in my journal to look up the Ted Talk while Tim rambled about the concept of power posing and how he thought it was so cool because it blended perfectly with what he was reading in the *Power of Now*. When he started to veer off topic into the world of Eckhart

Tolle, Julie patiently waited for a pause to guide him back to the golf story of the day.

"So did you practice the power-posing on the golf course today?"

"Oh Oh! Yeah! I did! The guys looked at me like I was crazy, but I told them I wanted to tee-off last. So the whole time while each of them teed-off, I stood like this!" Tim stopped flitting about the pool deck and stood firm on his feet with his arms in the air in a sort of superhero pose.

"You look like a superhero!" Julie proclaimed.

"That's the idea!" Tim announced as his voice lifted in excitement like a little kid. "I didn't care what the guys thought of me, I just wanted to see what would happen. Oh! Wait, I did more than just the power-posing! I did the deep breathing that my therapist has been teaching me." Julie looked at me and smiled again.

"So what happened when it was your turn to tee-off?"

"I hit the ball harder and farther than I ever have before!" As he finished his sentence, he did a little jump, like a little kid would, a jump of excitement about his story.

"You gotta try this TeriLeigh. I bet it'll make you feel better. Get up! Be Wonder Woman!" although I didn't feel much like Wonder Woman, I followed his lead and stood up and put my hands on my hips.

"You are a Rock Star!" Tim coached me. "Don't forget to breathe!" My non-yoga practicing military-vet friend was teaching me, the yoga teacher, about breathing.

"You gotta stay here for two minutes for it to work. Just keep breathing." He looked at his watch, and counted to me every twenty seconds, reminding me to breathe and to think like a super hero. And gosh darnit if it didn't work. I felt a little bit like a super hero when he high fived me at the end of two minutes.

"Did you teach the guys on the golf course what you were doing?" I asked, my chest feeling a little puffier than usual.

"Nah. They weren't having any of it. They just poked fun at me while I did it. But they noticed when I hit the ball as well as I did every single time!"

"Honey, isn't it time for you and Millie to go to work?" Julie said, handing Tim Millie's leash. Millie hopped off the chaise lounge and stretched a good long down dog and up dog.

"Oh yeah. Millie! It's time to go!" She circled around in excitement a few times before settling down to let Tim leash her up and lead her out the door. Just like that, my super hero coach and his furry sidekick were out the door.

A couple times a week, both during their three months snow-birding in Florida and their nine months in Minnesota, Tim and Millie volunteered as Peer Support Workers at the VA.

I was just one of many individuals on Millie's therapy-dog case load. She had a full docket of clients needing her care. Most of them were one-ups she met at the VA, people she met once and moved on. I was a passer-through. One she served for a short time, and then I moved on. But always, Millie's top priority and first patient was her own human, Tim. A marine corps vet who came home from Vietnam in the 1970s, Tim lived a full and happy life, until he retired and the hidden symptoms of post-traumatic stress were no longer so hidden.

Before I left teaching high school, nearly a decade before Fuck You Sunday, Ted and I taught high school together in the same building as Tim. Not only was Tim one of the most favorite teachers of all the students, but he was also considered the most happy-go-lucky member of the faculty, and the most sought after mentor. With his very clean and honest sense of humor, he often chaired the staff variety show committee, coming up with all kinds of ways to make the kids laugh with clean-humor spoofs on SNL skits.

For over 30 years, the atrocities Tim had endured in the war remained buried in the shadowed folds of his brain while he spent his days living in the busy-ness and lightness of everyday life. Having returned from the horrors of Vietnam to a healthy environment, a loving family, an adoring wife, and a steady and fulfilling career, the traumatic energies from Vietnam went dormant in his system for many years. School functions, family outings, and career success kept him busy and happy.

Then he retired.

When his world slowed down and distractions lessened, the memories of the war emerged. Sometimes in nightmares, other times in constant spinning and ticking and tripping of flashes of thought. When the energy in Tim's body shifted with the quieter lifestyle of retirement, the demons that had taken residence in deep recesses of his body could come out of their caverns. Tim started exhibiting severe symptoms of significantly delayed post-traumatic-stress from his time in Vietnam.

Julie did what she could to support Tim through emergencies and traumas of post traumatic stress as if she were slaying the beasts in the Vietnamese jungles with him. Millie smelled Tim's distress and instituted the *lab lean* and other healing tactics she instinctively knew. But together, Millie and Julie weren't enough to exorcise Tim's demons. During those first years of retirement, as Julie studied yoga with me, she tried and tried many times to coax Tim into the practice for his own healing. It wasn't until she led him to the VA where a seasoned therapist offered him yogic practices disguised as psychotherapy exercises.

As Tim told us about power-posing the morning, he was only beginning to recognize that all the things that were working for him were similar to the yoga, meditation, mindfulness and breathing practices I had been teaching Julie for years..

At the VA, Tim and Millie's job was to visit patients in the psych ward. There, patients who had been admitted for emergency situations often refused the treatments offered in the forms of therapy and mental health counseling. Many of the patients who came in as a result of temporary psychotic breaks refused to speak to anyone, at all, ever. Millie's job was to open the door to conversation, and Tim's job was to gently coax the patients to try the therapy counseling services offered by the VA.

Tim followed Millie's lead each time they entered the psych ward. She always knew just who in the room needed her the most that day. Sometimes, the person Millie went to was not even a patient, but a staff member who was particularly strained by the stresses of the job that day. Inevitably, someone who hadn't spoken for days, or at all, would pet Millie on the head and willingly engage in a conversation with Tim about dogs. Tim would then gently ease the conversation towards telling his own stories about dealing with post-traumatic stress. Millie worked to keep levels of anxiety and fears low, absorbing pain and stress through the pets and scratches.

While Tim and Millie were at the VA, Julie and I took Semper on a long walk to the nature preserve where manatees often gather. We talked about Tim's exuberance in telling stories and how he had completely embraced the yogic concepts of living in the present moment without even knowing it was yoga.

The Gift Inside the Wound

"Look at those manatees drinking water over there in the shallow water! They are so cute with their teddy bear faces!" Julie exclaimed.

Her own playfulness matching that of Tim's during his power-posing golf story. At just that moment, Semper lunged at me in the sand, and I found myself in a sandy beach wrestling match with a Labrador retriever. I laughed so hard I could barely breathe. When I finally did come up for air, I was consumed with gratitude.

"Thank you Julie. You and Tim and Millie and Semper are just the medicine I need."

For the next several days I let Julie and Tim, and Millie and Semper apply layer after layer of bandages to all of my wounds. Julie's home-cooked meals sealed the holes in my belly with a newfound appetite. Tim's excitement in the moment wrapped my heart with happiness. Millie's *lab leans* sealed my skin of all escaping coldness. And Semper's wrestles colored my casts with giggles. When I went to bed on my last night at Tim & Julie's, I realized that was the first day since Fuck You Sunday that I didn't cry.

Teri Leigh

THE GIFT

Teri Leigh

Time to Heal ~ Turning Within

The Gift Inside the Wound

Solitude and a Long Stretch of Alone Time

"I never found a companion that was so companionable as solitude."
~Henry David Thoreau

After a week on Millie's case load, I felt warm and loved. The Doble family bandages on my wounds made me feel protected, safe. I thought I was able to face the big bad world on my own once again.

Settled into the driver's seat, I checked my itinerary before driving off to my next destination. Half of the events I had booked fell through over the last month. I took a deep breath and remembered Julie's comment about something bigger being in charge. I didn't have control over these events and whether they cancelled or not. I didn't have time to be afraid. Besides, I had a much bigger fear standing in front of me.

The long stretch of alone time.
I had to drive from Florida to Vermont.

While I knew I'd be able to stay with friends all along the way, I also knew they were all busy with their normal every day work and family lives, and would have little time to entertain me or tend to my wounds as the Doble family did.

I started my car, blared the stereo with my favorite playlist and started the trek up the east coast. Before driving away, I looked over to the passenger seat, consciously inviting Grief to get back in as my co-pilot.

Grief had given up shotgun seat and slithered himself into the backseat of my mind. My passenger seat remained empty, but not for long.

Within the first 50 miles, between the vibrations of my car speakers and gentle rumblings of the road beneath me, I met Grief's sidekick.

Solitude.

Solitude buckled herself into the passenger seat with her bare feet up on the dash. She wore holey yoga pants and a stained t-shirt with no bra. She sang along to the music at the top of her lungs, sorely out of tune. Eating Pringles and spilling gummy bears between the seats, she flossed her teeth at the stoplights. While her hygiene and mannerisms were way outside my comfort zone, she definitely had a few things to teach me about the values of time spent alone.

Every morning, no matter where I was on the road, she prodded me to stop for coffee. She wouldn't settle for gas station coffee in a to-go cup. She required that I find a real coffee shop. Solitude buttoned an invisibility cloak at my neck before I walked away from the car. I'd take the hood off just enough to order my coffee, but then put it back on to shut out the outside world as I'd have full-on deep spiritual and reflective conversations with myself in my journal.

Once the conversation died down, Solitude tugged at my elbow and pulled me back to the car, where I felt most at peace. My Prius was the closest thing to a home I had. Each time I reached a destination, whether it was the fancy townhome of a client in North Carolina, or the breakfast I had with an old college friend in Baltimore, or a sorority sister's flat in New York, or the yoga studio in Vermont some 1500 miles later, Solitude prodded me to take a moment to prepare myself to be with other people before I could get out of my car and leave her behind.

At the same time, Solitude afforded me the opportunity to really enjoy the single life, to release of all compromises I conditioned myself to make.

How many times had I compromised things I wanted for Ted, or for others for that matter? How often in my life did I put the desires and feelings and experiences of others ahead of my own?

While in the safe and secure quiet little bubble of my car, I didn't have to think about compromising myself for anyone. Instead, I got to spend time, a lot of time, contemplating what my desires and feelings and experiences were. And because there was no one else around, I didn't have a choice but to put myself first.

And it felt good.

It felt REALLY GOOD.

I discovered an odd comfort in the process of just driving, like I really didn't care to reach my destination. There was a time in my life when driving meant a rush to get from one place to the next, like I couldn't get to my destination fast enough, like I just wanted the ride to be over. But on that trek, the heated seat beneath me felt like my pillow when I didn't want to get out of bed. The hum of the road under the tires was comforting, like vibrations that remind me I'm alive, like the sound of my own breath.

While Solitude warmed me through the heated seat of my car, every once in awhile, Loneliness would blow icy cold air in my face from the vent. I danced the razor's edge between these two emotions. Solitude was warm and cozy. Loneliness was cold and empty. Solitude was fulfilling, while loneliness left me hungry. A hunger pang or a gust of cold air sent sensations through my body turning the sweet cooing of solitude into the piercing echo of loneliness.

Being on the "divorce diet" I had absolutely no appetite for anything, much less the junk food that gas stations and rest stops had to offer. Unable to find nourishing food at rest stops and gas stations, I ignored my appetite in hopes that once I reached my destination someone on the other end would fill me with a home cooked meal and homegrown love.

But if I went too long without food, the hunger would fester from a hunger for food to a hunger for other things. This would remind me of the hunger I felt for Ted's companionship, and the emptiness with which he often greeted me. Ted had lived with various forms of eating disorders for the better part of thirty-five years. His normal state of being was balancing on the edge of emptiness. It was what he knew and found familiar and comfortable. He translated that hunger into a hunger for knowledge and spiritual liberation, and it served him well in his scriptural studies. He fed himself with books and contemplation, and thus didn't have room in his system for food, which made him feel dense and heavy. Hunger was a foreign experience to me, one that left me feeling weightless and floaty, ungrounded and unsafe. Our marriage, to me, was safety and security, my ground. To him, our marriage was confining and restrictive, his prison.

My marriage was like a ceramic cup filled with things like companionship, compromise, comfort, and coziness. While it was full, it was also deeply lonely, and thus sometimes felt claustrophobic. In his desire for space and freedom from the density and heaviness that I brought into the relationship, Ted took that cup and smashed it into the earth so that I couldn't walk barefoot on the ground anymore without getting shards stuck in my soles, and I was forced into a place of feeling weightless and floaty all the time.

I had to redefine what was my ground, my security. I made the conscious choice to step off the wing of the plane and embark on this journey alone, not running to one person to take care of me, but allowing many to give me little pushes to stand on my own feet along the way.

It was damn scary to not have anything outside myself to ground me. Could I be happy without someone to hold my hand? What would it be like to not have someone to crawl into bed with me at night? How would I feel if I didn't have someone to check in with me each day, to make sure I'm okay, and to hear the stories of my day?

Then there it was, a great big fear, riding on the hunger pains in my belly and the cold air on my face one of my greatest fears of life, like a flashing red warning light on the dashboard of the car. What if something happened to me, and I died alone and no one I knew or cared about heard about it for days?

The thought of dying alone bounced around inside my empty belly, ricocheting around in the vacuous space leaving loud echoes like in a racquetball court. Each lonely thought hit hard and loud, drowning out the soft soothing rumbling of solitude from the road below. One bounce, one thought would lead to another bounce and another thought, and so forth and so on, seemingly unending.

It started innocently enough, with thoughts of gratitude for being clear that I didn't want to be married to Ted anymore. Living with him was like living in a black hole. On the rim a reflection, a fold of my energy over and onto itself, that was actually somewhat beautiful. I liked the bounce of colors and light in refraction back to me. But after some time, I realized that it was just me being reflected back to me, and that he wasn't offering any substance himself. By that time, I was deeper into the thoughts, and thus deeper into the black hole. I recognized that in this space everything I put into the relationship was no longer reflected back but was just swallowed up, absorbed, like some strange wormhole in a Star Trek episode. On the next level, the next bounce, I felt like what I offered was not being received, nor was it used for nourishment, it just disintegrated, evaporated. The more I gave, the more it evaporated, leaving me depleted and even more hungry. I was left with no means with which to relate to Ted because he was nothing, empty, a black hole.

Whatever emotion I threw at him came back as an empty stare from his ice blue eyes, a vast void. While I was clear that I didn't want to live with Ted anymore because the empty black hole was so cold and vacuous, the biggest hit of the racquetball thoughts in my head came with a loud grumble of my hungry stomach. What if I had gone so far down the hole with Ted that nothing I offered was received by anyone or anything? What if everything I had to give was disintegrated by everyone and everything?

Again, my body tried to tell me what I needed by filling up the space in my skull with fluid, by the squeeze of grief and sadness on my throat. And the tears emerged. So I cried, yet, I still felt empty. The fullness of the wetness of my being wasn't enough.

I was hungry.

When I eventually stopped for gas and sucked on a dark chocolate snickers bar with the heat on full blast in my car, I asked myself the question again. What if something happened to me, and I died alone? What if no one I knew or cared about heard about my death for days? Having filled my belly and warmed my tissues, the coin of loneliness flipped as quickly as it had appeared.

Solitude winked at me, "What do you care? You'd be dead."

And just like that, the quivers of my sobs became bounces of my laughter.

What I recognized after finishing my candy bar was that the feelings that came with hunger are as fleeting as the feelings that came with comfort. My comfort with Ted went *poof* on Fuck You Sunday as quickly as my anxiety of being empty went *poof* after eating some chocolate. Things change. How I feel about those things changes too.

But underneath all of that, there was this tiny piece of myself that didn't change, that piece of myself that was choosing to have the experience of it all, good and bad.

What is good and bad anyway? One of my favorite quotes has always been "there is no right or wrong, only right or left." I tend to think of right as good and wrong as bad, but if I reframed those words as right and left, good and bad are as changeable as pleasure and pain.

In looking back through all the emotions I had experienced in the last two months (was that all it was? Two months? Gosh, things can change so much in such little time) that tiny piece of me that is happy to be human and having this experience was really blissful that I had the opportunity to feel all those emotions.

Underneath it all, there was a piece of me that was happy I got to feel sadness at the Minnesota cabin. There was a piece of me that was happy that I got to feel anxiety in the Iowa hotel. There was a piece of me that was happy I got to feel cold in the Florida sun. What I realized on that long drive between Loneliness and Solitude was that had I not felt those emotions, I wouldn't have been able to flip the coin of each one and feel the opposite either. Because I knew Sadness, I also knew great Happiness. Because I knew Anxiety, I knew Peace. Because I knew Cold, I knew Warmth. But moreso, because I knew that none of them was permanent, and each of them was a balance of the opposite, I knew that I was alive, experiencing my humanness at its fullest.

Love is a State of Being

"Love is energy of life."
~Robert Browning

Several states, and dinner tables, and guest bedrooms later, I drove into the Green Mountains of Vermont where I was to lead the chakra portion of a yoga teacher training. The snow and sleet was thick, caking a huge sheet of ice onto the front of my car. For many miles, I followed a semi truck bearing the name *Swift*.

Oddly, I felt swift in my little Prius, skating through the snowflakes.

I felt like I was the air passing through the elements of the environment. While I drove, I let Solitude coax me into singing out loud. I felt the back of my throat open, a tunnel that started with a pressure at the back of my tongue and first connected to my diaphragm and then down to my naval, and finally to my tailbone. My voice echoed a loud heavy vibration, like a rumbling sheet of metal.

As I sang, an anger came over me. Rather, a fierce rage consumed me. I was angry at myself, at Ted, and at every single person in my life who had allowed me to compromise too much of myself for them. I wanted to break the strings and chains knotted around me in the bonds of these relationships.

At the end of the CD, as the ferocity in me transformed into resolve, Solitude coaxed me to stop at a lookout on the side of a mountain. When I got out of the car, I shrugged my shoulders and shook my upper body as if I were shaking my wings open. I looked over the railing at the ledge of the cliff, yearning to fly. Closing my eyes, I imagined the soft gossamer strings that wrapped around my wings keeping them pinned to my body drop to the earth. In that moment, that tiny imagination off the edge of a mountain, all my past evaporated. The relationships I had held and nurtured, those I had cared for, putting their needs before my own – I let go of their hands and spread my wings.

And then with a deep breath, I launched, both light and strong, a solidness that was held by the depth of my voice. For several breaths, I let the cold snowy wind brush me away, and I floated on the wings of my imagination into the independent sky.

When I did finally open my eyes, Solitude beckoned me to a trailhead at the other end of the parking lot. I knew I had to walk more, feeling solid and stronger on my feet than I ever had before. Being deeper in my voice and taller in my stance, my heart pumped fuller and louder as I climbed. My blood felt darker, thicker, almost black. A huntress, stalking through the snow, I was eager to slaughter anything that threatened to chain and bind me again.

About a quarter mile up the trail, I came across a mountain stream. Veering off trail, I climbed up a few feet into the woods to get to the edge of the stream. In the winter cold, I shed my shoes and socks and plunged my feet into the water. The water was ice cold, so cold that within ten seconds of dropping my soles in the stream, I felt a chilling pain climb up my legs.

I felt as though the water had penetrated through my heel bone and was snaking its way up my leg through the marrow of my bones, crystallizing my tissues as it climbed. At first, I squealed at the sensation. The chill of the water rushed through every pore of my being. The iciness of the water made it feel cleaner, crisper, and thus made me feel more pure, vibrant, alive.

I imagined the water not as ice crystals, but as little electrical impulses stimulating every part of my feet and legs. The cold instantly turned to heat, and I felt almost burned by the chill. I felt awake, alive, vibrant and vivid.

Barefoot, I walked down the stream, over rocks, across twigs, letting my feet sink deep into the icy water and the soft muddy stream bed. The cold flushed over my toes and soles, washing away my fears, grounding me into the deep vibrations I had evoked with my voice just moments before.

Several yards upstream, I came to a tiny clearing in the woods where I could see over the mountains and valleys. I looked out over the snow-capped evergreen trees and realized just how far I had come since walking across the bitter cold Minnesota lake not too many weeks ago. The cold water rushing over my feet, zapping them with warm electricity, the Anger I had felt just down the trail had shape-shifted into Passion.

Passion squeezed at my heart, which pumped harder through the fist of her grip. I yearned to run, to drive, to GO. I wanted to go anywhere, to run and not look back. I wanted to get somewhere else, anywhere else than where I had been. My heart pumping so hard, I felt as though it might push itself right outside of my winter coat.

Then, Solitude beckoned me to return to the car. Eagerly, she was anxious and excited to finish the drive to my next job.

Once I tugged my shoes and socks back on, I bounced down the mountain trail, half running, half skipping, half leaping. Like Tigger, my legs sometimes trailed far behind me as I bounced through the mountain woods.

My first day teaching the yoga teacher training, students peppered me with questions about my background, my experience, my training. And then, as almost always happens, one student became uncharacteristically vulnerable and changed the course of the conversation from curiosity about me to deep self-inquiry.

"Can you talk for a minute about anger? I can't seem to make mine go away. It feels like it is keeping me away from feeling love. As much as I think about peace and happiness, I can't get the anger to go away."

How synchronistic that just the day before I had let Anger take my steering wheel and watched him veer me off course to meet Passion. Before the student could finish her question, my heart was pounding as it had when I imagined my wings open at the mountain stream just the day before.

As often happens when I teach, my voice started speaking without my brain thinking. My throat opened as it had when I was singing out loud with Solitude in my car. Contents of my experiences spilled out uncontrollably out of my mouth, yet in an articulate and organized fashion. Her question triggered the wisdom of all my ancestors that resided deep in the marrow of my bones. I felt as though their voices culminated into the vibrations of my vocal chords, and I was just a marionette to their musings.

"I like Anger!" I said excitedly.

"I hope you can find a way to become friends with Anger, because he can be your greatest asset!" I lept out of my half lotus pose on the yoga bolster, filled with excitement for her.

"Anger is a very necessary part of any growth process, and should not be shunned, but MUST be validated and appreciated! Anger is part of being human. If you deny it, you are invalidating a part of yourself. That part of yourself MUST be acknowledged. If you sweep it under the rug or treat it like it's undesirable, it will only grow louder, and louder! Anger is like the mischievous child who needs attention. Anger is just left of passion, a pivot, a flip, and turn-key away from the deepest expression of love."

At this point, I could no longer pay attention to whether the class was listening or not. I paced and bounced around the room as I spoke. Their eyes followed, somewhat mesmerized by my animation, but I had not a clue if they really heard anything I was saying.

"Anger is an emotion. It's fleeting. It always eventually passes, transforms, shape-shifts, and changes. It can either morph into rage and wreak havoc. Or, if you work with it, anger helps you make changes in your life, in your world. When harnessed, Anger is Transformation.

"Harnessed Anger is what fueled the civil rights movement of the 1960s. Harnessed Anger is what fed the Civil War eventually leading to the Emancipation Proclamation. Harnessed Anger is what got women the right to vote. Ghandi harnessed Anger against the British. Nelson Mandela harnessed his Anger while in prison and eventually abolished Apartheid and become President. Harnessed Anger Causes Change!"

I took a moment, sat back down on the bolster. The class was entranced. Speechless.

I took a deep breath as I felt Passion squeeze again on my heart. She wanted me to share about Fuck You Sunday. I felt the story bubble up through my throat. It was different than the frog in my throat cat got my tongue feeling that I'd gotten so used to happening before I would cry. This was more of a need to burp.

Was this really wise, to share my raw story with my students? But her fist squeezed and pushed until everything just came gushing out.

The class was silent, so I continued.

"Let me make this more personal for you. The lesson I'm trying to teach you here, it's very raw and fresh for me. I am only just experiencing this myself as I'm in the middle of my own process of harnessing Anger. Just two months ago, my husband of 10 years told me he wants to be a celibate monk."

Although I didn't actually burp, it felt like a huge gas bubble erupted out of my mouth, and with it, the class gasped. The words in my throat didn't give me or the students any time to let the beginning of the story land. The story of Fuck You Sunday just spilled out, like the silverware falling out of a broken kitchen drawer, clinking and clattering, and sprinkling ding sounds all over the room.

When I finished telling the story, and how I packed up and went on the road, one of the students choked out a question.

"How are you even here right now?"

"That, my friends, is the power of harnessing Anger to provoke CHANGE! Ted spit his Anger darts at me, and that was what I needed to create a massive schism in my system. It shattered me. It shifted me. When I got up off that floor from behind that chair, the Anger he had spit at me consumed ME. I got angry. Mind you, I wasn't rage-ful like he was, I was ANGRY. I used that Anger to make a massive change in my life that I wouldn't even consider before."

I sat back down, took a gulp of water, and felt it splash into my stomach like a boulder in a still pond. Just talking about Fuck You Sunday and the memories constricted into my belly. The knots, the strength, the conviction, the purpose, the ANGER.

"Come to think of it, every single time I even think about what it felt like to be looking up at him from the floor behind that chair I feel it, the schism, the shift. The Transformation. It's this intense undeniable unforgiveable desire for something different...anything different! That's how I'm here right now. This here is different than being there with him.

"I've covered 20 states in two months. That's different than anything I've ever done before. Calling people and asking for help, letting them pay for my meals, put me up in their homes, take care of me when I usually take care of them. That's different for me. Harnessing the Anger made me take risks and do things I wouldn't have otherwise done. And to tell you the truth, as terrifying as it is, it's a helluva lot of fun!"

The class laughed. I was on a roll. Time seemed to slow down, the clocks ticking drowned and stopped by the clatter of my story.

"Now, back to your original question," I looked the woman in the eye, "This is very important!"

Crouching down to the floor, I slapped my open-faced hand onto the wood planked floor so they could feel the vibration. And then I whispered, "You must understand, Anger does not cancel nor block nor invalidate Love. They can and MUST coexist. As angry as Ted was at me, as Angry as I was with him and the situation, it never canceled out the love we had, and probably will always have for each other."

Then, I sat back down on my yoga bolster, wrapped my feet up underneath me in half lotus pose. The burps heaving from my heart into my throat softened into happy little effervescent bubbles.

"Let me explain to you what I've learned about love, what it really is, and even offer you a scientific explanation. And then I'll let you go to lunch. Do you need a little break? Does anyone need a little snack?"

No one moved.

"Don't stop."

"Tell us."

I continued.

"Love is not just an emotion. Love is so much more. Love is a state of being. Let me say that again. Love. Is. A. State. Of. Being. Love is the condition of existence, of being connected to all things and all beings through the mutual exchange of molecules and energy."

The circle of yogis leaned in to hear me. I saw cartoon stars in their eyes, spinning a trance-like quality in their minds. My voice settled into a natural volume, and steady rhythm, a cadence.

"Our bodies are made up of atoms, molecules, and particles. You might remember this from fifth grade science, or maybe even high school chemistry class."

"This is the nucleus of an atom, made up of protons and neutrons," I made a fist with my left hand.

"Spinning around that nucleus are electrons. How many electrons and how they spin determine what type of atom on the periodic table of elements," I circled my fist with my pointer finger of my right hand.

"When two atoms combine to make a molecule, they share electrons," I made a figure eight symbol of my right hand pointer finger revolving around my fist and around another imaginary fist in the air.

"More molecules combine by more electrons spinning and sharing to make bigger particles of matter."

"Does this all sound familiar?" The class nodded their heads.

"Energy is what moves those electrons around. Energy is what makes them jump ship and attach to other atoms and form or break molecules. Energy is neither created nor destroyed. It simply changes form. Get it!?"

I got very animated at this point. I knew I was getting to the punch line, and I was very excited to see how they took the news.

"When an atom meets another atom to form a molecule, there's an attraction. And then they SHARE electrons and join together. Doesn't that sound like LOVE?! Love is not a mood or an emotion. It is the energy of sharing electrons! Love is ENERGY. Love is the constant changing and shifting and moving of atoms and molecules. Love is that state of being, of all things!"

I took a pause. Did they get it? They were mesmerized. I needed to slow down just a bit so they didn't drink my lesson too quickly. I didn't want their brains to get overwhelmed like the feeling of drinking a carbonated beverage and laughing so it shoots up your nose into your sinuses. I wanted them to take the information in little sips, so that it wouldn't belch right back out of them before they fully digested it. But, I didn't want to stop for too long, as I had more bubbles piling up at the back of my throat.

"Some parts, like our bones and tissues are more dense than others, but it's all the same stuff. The vibration and exchange of those particles amongst all things on the planet is what love is. Love is constantly changing form. You are breathing in energy coming out of me right now. In fact, you're breathing in the molecules and oxygen atoms shared by countless people who have been in this room before you. That's love! There is mathematical research to prove that right now you are breathing at least some of the energy of Caesar's last breath. Google it…Caesar's last breath."

A handful of students scribbled the words Caesar's last breath on their notebooks. I stood up again, and stomped my foot into the floor again.

"Love is NOT an emotion that is subject to the production and processing of hormones and enzymes in the body. Your other moods and emotions are built around hormones and enzymes. Love is a vibration, an energy. It cannot be blocked or barricaded or canceled or invalidated. It is ALWAYS present. You just have to acknowledge it, notice it, accept it, recognize that LOVE is the vibration of all other emotions!"

I looked back at the student who asked the original question about how to deal with anger over love.

"Your Anger is perfectly valid, and necessary. And it's a GOOD THING! It's gonna help you transform energy into a different form. And it's changing your hormones and enzymes in your body to make your energy, your LOVE move faster, bigger, different, MORE! Your anger is just an expression of your love!

"As is your lust, and attraction, and kindness, and loneliness, and fear, and passion. All feelings are expressions of LOVE. All emotions are different faces, vibrations, and movements of LOVE! Go ahead, feel your Anger. Harness it. It is showing you HOW MUCH LOVE YOU HAVE. It's making you find a new and different transformed way of expressing your love."

Passion squeezed on my heart again, and I felt that familiar ice pick sensation. She wanted me to bring it back around to my personal story, to Fuck You Sunday.

"I will always love my husband. But the way our love was moving was stagnant. Together, we had changed our vibration so much, learning and growing and playing in those electrons together. Our energy, our love got so big that we couldn't be stuck together anymore. It needed to grow. Our love had outgrown our chemical bonding connection. Our electrons couldn't stay connected anymore because they were vibrating differently now. Ted brought me to where and who and how I vibrate now. That will never change. That's love. And letting go of the bonds that tied and constricted and held each other back…that's even deeper love."

I sat down again. I was whispering again, wetness spilling down my cheeks as fast as the words tumbled out of my mouth.

The Gift Inside the Wound

"This is the last thing I'll say. The point is not to get rid of Anger, but to feel it, to experience it, to know it, and to recognize that it does not, in any way shape or form, impact one's capacity for love because love is ever-present while anger is just a temporary way of expressing love. Yoga is a practice we do to remember this fact. We do yoga to feel and process the emotions of life through our physical bodies while at the same time remembering the ultimate state of love as the underlying Truth of who we are."

When I was done, I said to the class, "Did you get that? Because I don't know where that came from or if I could even repeat it."

I sat down back on my bolster cushion in half-lotus. Half exhausted, but mostly exhilarated.

All eyes looked right at me.

No. Actually, they all looked right into me.

There was a really long silence.

The room was buzzing in silence.

Finally, the woman who had asked the question broke the silence. She had been crying for most of my lecture, but hadn't bothered to wipe the tears as they streaked her cheeks.

"Thank you," she said, "That was the most beautiful explanation of yoga and the meaning of love that I have ever heard."

Teri Leigh

Removing the Bandages ~ Moving Forward

The Gift Inside the Wound

A Different Point of View

*"If you change the way you look at things,
the things you look at change."*
~Dr. Wayne Dyer

Rob is a dear friend whom I'd meet whenever I passed through New York City. He took great pleasure in giving me experiences that I wouldn't otherwise have as a suburban Midwesterner. Over my years of travel, meeting him in New York City several times, we shared cocktails at a quaint wine bar in Central Park. He'd shown me how to hail a cab in Manhattan during rush hour. He'd taught me how to order the finest cut of meat in a fancy steakhouse. He'd open doors for me, and put his hand lightly on my back as I walked through. Never once had he ever allowed me to even come close to reaching for my wallet to pay a tab or tip a cabbie.

Back in January, when I'd booked my flight to Maui out of JFK, I contacted Rob in hopes of having another platonic tryst with my gay boyfriend.

He invited me to join him and his sister at The View Restaurant and Lounge, a rotating restaurant located 48 floors up with stunning views of the Manhattan skyline. He insisted he would give me a different point of view than I had ever seen before. Although he was talking about the city landscape from the top of a skyscraper, I somehow knew the experience would change my perspective on other things as well.

Looking out over the city, I recognized an odd symbolism in the city lights. I was the city. Every light was a popped pore of my skin, a tiny wound of my being, a story of my life and my experience pouring out of me. Under every twinkling light was a person having an experience, bandaging a wound, tending to a scar, or nursing a trauma. Their pains were my pains. At the same time, each light twinkled with joys, and celebrations, happiness, and pleasure.

My entire life had shifted on Fuck You, Sunday. Standing there at the window of this restaurant suspended in the sky, I somehow knew how Alice felt in the rabbit hole, and how Dorothy felt in the tornado. I emerged from the north woods cabin welcomed by the munchkins and mad-hatters of my own Wonderland of Oz.

Rob fit right into my mystical musings, wearing nicely buffed wing tip shoes, skin-tight candy-apple red pants, and an overly embroidered white linen shirt. Every word he spoke, he enunciated with a tickle of glee, like the twirl off the top of the munchkin's hat or the flip of the foot of the white rabbit's hop.

"I cannot believe you finally get to meet my sister! I'm so glad you're here!" Rob gushed excitement and gratitude as he hugged me hello.

The host offered us our reserved table on the inner tier of the restaurant, and Rob adamantly refused.

"Oh no! We can't have that! This beauty here has come thousands of miles to see me."

Rob wrapped his arm around my shoulder and squeezed me just a bit too tight. He wrapped his other arm around his sister's waist and pulled her into him.

"And this is my sister, the most precious person in my life."

"I simply MUST give these ladies the full experience. Wouldn't you agree?"

"Would you like to wait for a window table?" The host asked politely.

"I'd have it no other way!" Rob said, "We'll just settle ourselves at the bar until a window table is ready."

"You do understand, Sir, that could be 30-45 minutes."

"We will wait. I'll have nothing but the best for my ladies." Rob grabbed us each by the hand, a firm grip, and led us to the bar.

Thirty minutes and six consecutive stories from Rob later, the host returned with a beautiful assistant to offer us a nicer table.

"May I carry your wine to your table for you?" the assistant asked. While my first instinct was to say no because I was more than capable of carrying my own wine, and the nice girl Midwesterner in me didn't want to put anyone out, I watched as Rob's sister nonchalantly handed the woman her glass.

Clearly, this dining experience was gifted to me to test my "yes, thank you" skills. I followed the example of Rob's sister, who carried herself with the same confidence and grace I learned from Olivia. I stood up a little taller, embraced empowerment, and surrendered my wine glass to the assistant.
"Yes, thank you," I said.
"May I take your jacket to our coat closet?"
"Yes, thank you."
"Would you like some bottled water?" Well of course, bottled and not tap water, duh.
"Yes, thank you."
"Sparkling or still?" Really, I had a choice?
"Still, thank you."
"May I offer you your napkin, Miss?" our waiter said as he flirted with me and winked at Rob simultaneously.
"Yes, thank you."

After a couple dozen more "yes, thank yous" in the midst of one of Rob's animated stories, while swallowing a very tasty bite of mahi mahi, I was overcome with gratitude. The mango salsa-covered fish coated my esophagus with this smooth softness that slid right down into my core. The tiny bite of ginger and jalapeño tickled my insides with butterfly flips of appreciation.

There I was, high up above Manhattan, living the high life, eating a meal that would cost me more than two days' pay, and I was completely consumed with happiness and gratitude and appreciation for the moment, the experience, the flavor of every sensation.

In all my grief, my loneliness, and solitude, one pervading question lodged so deep in the pit of my gut that I was so afraid to verbalize that I wouldn't even admit it in my journal. Deep down, I was constantly wondering...

Am I not good enough?

If Ted, my husband and the love of my life could just throw me away like the last bites of his anorexic meals, would I ever be good enough for anyone else?

Rob showed me that not only was I good enough…
I was fabulous, and I deserved it!

Moreso, Rob had showed me the cozy comfortable space that lives between Loneliness and Solitude. He showed me how to be comfortable with being completely myself in his presence, and to accept and say "yes, thank you" to being ME.

"Would you like dessert?" our server asked, lifting the last plate off the table.
"That's a silly question," Rob said to the server. "Of course we do!"
"Yes, thank you."

After dessert and the bill had been paid, I stood up to hug Rob and thank him.
"Did you enjoy your meal?" He asked as I wrapped my arms around him.
"Yes, thank you," and I held him, squeezed him, and placed my hand flat open-palmed in the center of his back heart. I wanted him to feel my gratitude and appreciation, every honey drop of it. When he started to pull away, I pulled him closer, held him tighter, and longer.
"Thank you….Thank you…Thank you…" I whispered in his ear. I wanted to tell him that for the first time in my life, I felt as beautiful as the compliments I received.
I wanted to tell him that for the first time in my world, I KNEW I was good enough, more than good enough. I wanted him to KNOW that in bringing me to that restaurant and giving me the red carpet treatment, I finally felt WORTHY. I wanted him to know that by showing me how to look at myself through his eyes, I was able to see myself differently. I wanted to tell him that he made it okay for me to take the bandages off…and keep them off.

But I had no words. So I just held him, and let him hold me.

When we finally did pull apart, we both had wetness in our eyes. I felt the top layer of bandages drop off, and I felt lighter.

Surrender and Let Go

"Don't turn your back on the ocean."
~Hawaiian saying

Wearing a different pair of glasses on my face after having seen a different point of view with Rob, I boarded a 10-hour flight from New York City to Honolulu. Because everything in my world had changed, I had a particularly deep ache for the familiar. I looked at my visit to Maui as a homecoming because it was the first time I would land in the arms of family since I cried in my Mother's arms the day of my wounding. But, I hadn't been to Maui in over five years. My brother had since gotten married to a beautiful young Thai woman, and many things on the island had changed.

Nothing was the same.
Nothing was familiar.

As I got off the plane, all I wanted was a hug from my little brother Dave. Dave's birthday is the day before mine, and he looks like the male version of me. If we ever had a DNA test done, I would guess that ours is almost identical. While he lives on Maui and has a much different lifestyle, Dave's perspective on life and his attitude towards experiences match mine closely. Spending time with him is often like spending time with the masculine version of myself.

As kids, we used to watch this super-hero cartoon where twin siblings would fist bump each other and a flash of light would ignite whatever super-power they chose to have for the task at hand. As an adult, I had come to enjoy a hug from Dave like that flash of light.

After all I'd been through, I wanted Dave to wrap me up in his arms and feel that flash of light.

Wonder-twin powers – ACTIVATE!

Except that, they didn't.

Dave put the lei around my neck, draping it evenly over my chest and back. He hugged me, but something was off. The energy wasn't the same. When he released the hug before I did and my wonder-twin-power didn't activate, I felt a heavy drop of sadness.

The cold chill of Grief's icy fingernails pressed into my lungs. The scars under my bandages began to throb. The scabs were stuck to the gauze, and I hesitated in my desire to expose my rawness to the world, even in the familiar home of my brother. I gasped, and then swallowed, pleading with Grief, *not here, not now, please, not now.*

Goy must've sensed my chill. Before I could exhale the sob that was frozen at the top of my throat, my brother's wife wrapped her petite feather soft arms around my waist, and pulled me into her tiny frame.

"Hello Sister," she whispered into my ear.

And I felt home.
Another layer of bandages unraveled from my sores.

The next morning, after sleeping off jetlag, while Dave and Goy were at work, Solitude led me to Twin Falls. The drive to Twin Falls is an easy meandering along Hana Highway, and the turn-off is obvious with a fruit stand guarded by a couple of large coconut figurines. It's a popular tourist spot where non-Hawaiians lounge by a pair of waterfalls that splash into a pool just a short easy hike behind the parking lot. Unbeknownst to most of the tourists, the hike continues on upwards into the hills to five other waterfalls, each one being a little more secluded and less populated. One has a shallow cavern behind the falls. Another has rock beds that look like Mother Nature formed them precisely to serve as sunbathing recliners. The hike increases in difficulty with each one. Tourists rarely make it beyond the first or second falls.

My first time in Maui, Dave led me up to the fifth waterfall where we were greeted by a sweet elderly hippie nudist couple. The man lounged by a tree next to the waterfall pool and played a wooden flute while the woman bathed in the pool. A small climb around some exposed root trees led to a rock on top of the waterfall that served as a perfect diving platform. The sun glinted off the waterfall pool in diamond reflections, and the sweet music of the flute echoed off the rocks and trees. Time stopped as we swam there, muted by the music of the flute, we barely spoke for over an hour while we frolicked there until our hunger forced us to leave the oasis and follow the dirt path back to the fruit stand for nourishment.

This time, with Solitude as my companion, I went in search of the fifth waterfall on my own. When I finally reached it, my heart sank just a little bit because I couldn't hear the flute music.

Seeing that I was alone, save the occasional song of a bird, I stepped out of my clothes to skinny dip. Just then, a couple of dogs, a corgi and a beagle, wandered down the path to drink from the pool. They sniffed around the perimeter as if they were doing their daily rounds, checking their messages, and moved on their way.

I let go of the nostalgia of the elderly hippie couple in order to embrace the experience of skinny-dipping with random pups. Next to my clothes on the rocks, I left another unravel of gauze bandages.

The next day, I drove through the fancy resort area of Maui to Makena Beach. The manicured lawns and pristine landscaping of the Fairmont and Four Seasons resorts, meandered through Wailea. They looked exactly like the resorts I had driven through in Naples, Florida a few weeks earlier, proving my theory that in trying to recreate something, it loses some of its power. In searching for home in Dave's hug and in the desire to hear the flute music at Twin Falls, I got lost in the sadness of nostalgia. But in driving through the fancy resorts, I realized that no matter how much 'the same' these fancy hotels made things, they would always be just that, a hotel; a place away from home.

When I got to Makena Beach, also known as Big Beach, the large waves scared me away from swimming, so I climbed the little ridge off to the side to get to the quieter Little Beach on the other side. A nudist beach, Little Beach was populated mostly by the stereotypical "dirty old man" with an occasional hippie couple and their naked babies playing in the sand. Having had a taste of skinny-dipping at Twin Falls, I wanted to enjoy the waters of the ocean sans bikini as well. Little Beach was quiet that day, less than a dozen beach towels and even fewer umbrellas.

Once I settled into a cozy spot on Little Beach, an old man walked by, buck naked from head to toe, except a fine gold watch. I suppose his watch was the one thing of value that he didn't want to leave behind, but to me it was symbolic of man's attachment to time and money. I looked down and noticed I was still wearing my watch, so I took it off and shoved it in the bottom of my beach bag.

I had a resistance to getting in the water because it might be cold. I had spent so long trying to get warm as I came out of the ice of Minnesota and my marriage to Ted, the last thing I wanted was to discover the cold was still there, hidden inside me. Or worse, would the salt sting my wounds just as I was removing the bandages, showing me I hadn't really healed much at all?

I took a cue from the naked curly-haired toddlers, and ran at full speed. I imagined I had tied my bandage to the rod of the umbrella and untangled myself from the gauze as I ran into the water. The chill only lasted a moment. Like a naked toddler, I giggled and splashed. I had ripped off more bandages, leaving the cruddy scab behind, and I completely ignored the sting and rip of pain in trade for the giggles and laughter and smiles that lived inside the surf, jumping over the breaking waves.

When I got out to where the waves weren't breaking, I rested on the cushion of the bobbing waves, I felt rocked and supported by the water, almost reminiscent of being submerged in the amniotic fluid of Mother Earth's womb.

"Remember, you can't push the ocean," a paddleboarder said as he paddled by. While it brings with it a great sense of joy and peace, the ocean is a powerful force that must be respected.

I floated on the rise of waves, balancing between surrendering to the wave yet not allowing myself to get pulled by the current. Through it's strong current, the ocean pushed me, forcing me to surrender to something I couldn't see, my future. All the while I kept an eye on the surf just enough to not let it take me away entirely. As I relinquished control mostly to the salty sea, I let more bandaging fall from my wounds.

Later that evening, I sat on the shore of Pa'ia Beach while Dave took to his surfboard. He stayed on the periphery, as if he is holding the container for the whole group. Other surfers would more often than not catch a wave and duck out early, as if they got bored and wanted to get back so as not to miss anything that might be more exciting over the next crest.

Dave, on the other hand, enjoyed every part of the process. He studied the wave and the surfers trying to catch it. Sometimes, he took more pleasure in watching someone else catch a wave and enjoy it than if he had caught it himself, humbly catching the reflection of someone else's glory as subtle, but more powerful, than his own glory.

To surf is to blend and merge with the circle of energy created by the wave, and for Dave, watching it happen to another is just as beautiful as doing it himself. Like watching a child realize they are riding a bicycle without anyone's help, watching someone pop up onto the board in full faith and trust in themselves and then merge with the elements around them into a full circle of energy is beautiful.

Dave could analyze the psychology of a crowd of surfers in just a few moments, recognizing who were the hungry ones that would force their way onto a wave, who were the newbies who didn't know the unspoken code, who were the timid ones who had the skill but not the confidence to catch the bigger rides, and who were the cocky ones that had the confidence but not the talent to catch the more dangerous curls.

Sometimes, he had more fun sitting on his board and watching the human dynamics interact with each other and how the natural dynamics of the waves and weather could shift the energy of the people over time.

At the same time, as a seasoned surfer, Dave is well aware of the ultimate surfing experience, to enter the barrel, to be completely inside the circle of water energy. As the spiral pulls one into the vortex, a deep resonant hum vibrates from the tumble of the water through the marrow of the bones. Dave once described it as the ultimate oneness experience, being fully consumed by the wave is like becoming fully enveloped by Mother Nature.

However, for Dave, most of his memorable surfing experiences didn't involve catching a wave at all, but involved some deeper interaction with nature. Over the years he had occasionally sent me photos or texts of his various encounters with nature.

"Got a little scared today. I think I went too far out on the surfboard as the whale was a little too close. Those things are massive!"

"Canoed with sea turtles today. You would've loved it."

That particular evening, too many immature surfers were hogging the shallow waves for Dave to enjoy his own rides, so he came back into shore and sat next to me on the beach and taught me about the human dynamics as they interacted with the natural elements. He then began to tell me one of the more dramatic stories of his surfing adventures when he took a lengthy drive to a somewhat rocky hike to a bay to surf at sunrise. Just on the outer lip of the bay was a pod of dolphins.

"I learned that day that it really takes very little intention to make something happen if you're willing to let go of your own attachment to what you want," Dave started his story about the dolphins.

"I went underwater at first just to see if I could hear them. Then, in just the tiniest flash of a thought, I sent the intention to communicate with them. I mean, it was just a tiny flash of a thought, just enough to tell them that I was listening. The next thing I knew, they completely surrounded me and circled me."

How many times in my life had I put forth great effort to make something happen? I'd set goals, and then set goals within those goals, and I wrote to-do lists and checked off the items on those lists.

Heck, I'd even applied the good old-fashioned Midwestern work ethic to making my marriage work. Where had it gotten me? Dolphins weren't circling me, that was for sure.

If I really stopped to think about it, I had a few of my own stories like Dave's dolphins, where I'd had the tiniest of thoughts and let go of them and somehow the stars seemed to align to create something even more miraculous than I could have imagined in my wildest dreams.

I taught this concept in my yoga classes, right effort, or in Sanskrit, stira-sukha balance. Sthira being the effort, and Sukha being the letting-go, the grace. I'd even named my dog Sukha in an effort to remind myself to let go of my willful grip on things. This whole adventure since leaving my home in Minnesota was one test after another forcing me to let go, to surrender my will, and to see what possibilities may evolve once I gave up my own vision and perception.

The water in Maui definitely douses any fire. I felt little to no motivation in myself, and a lot of ease and flow. At the same time, living on Maui-time was very exhausting, heavy even, to just be on the beach and not want to go or do anything.

I suppose this is why beach vacations are so restful, because people are forced by the water into a state of inaction and moving slow. People come to Hawaii for vacation and renew themselves for the "real world" for just a couple weeks at a time. My "real world" was changing so quickly that being in Maui didn't feel like a vacation to rejuvenate myself to go back to my life, as much as it was a cleansing to prepare me for my new world.

The cleansing served to douse my fire, to help me let go of my willfulness. This meant that I also had to let go of knowing exactly what my next step would be.

Teri Leigh

Look Up and Have Faith

"Faith is taking the first step even when you don't see the whole staircase."
~Martin Luther King, Jr

The next day, Dave took me for a hike in the bamboo forest. What I didn't know was that he was taking me through a ritual that taught him to let go of control in hopes that it would help me.

Wonder twin powers, activate.

The beginning of the hike was familiar, with solid earthy paths weaving in between thousands of huge crisp stalks of bamboo that climbed like Jack's Beanstalk into the sky. Ever since I was a little girl, I've loved the look of bamboo. In art class as a kid, I did a Zen painting of bamboo that my mother had framed and hung in our entryway, my only piece of artwork that went beyond stick figures and childish drawings.

Bamboo was always my flooring of choice for underneath my yoga mat. Recently, I'd even taken to buying clothing made of the soft bamboo fabric. One of my favorite qualities of bamboo is the symbolism of how the leaves grow. The younger branches at the top of the bamboo trunk grow in a way that allows the sunlight to reach the older branches below. At the same time, when young shoots grow out of the roots, they grow under the shade of the elder shoots above. Walking amongst the bamboo was comforting to me, like walking amongst a forest of very wise beings.

The path led to a river, which made my heart sing a little because I knew well that skipping along river rocks behind Dave was guaranteed to bring me to a waterfall pool, or two, or in this case, three.

The first pool came just after we emerged from the bamboo forest and was a cool easy swim with a couple other locals taking a morning splash before heading off to their restaurant jobs later that afternoon. Alongside that pool was a well-worn rope ladder. Dave scaled the rope ladder along the rock wall with ease in his slippahs, the Hawaiian term for flip-flops.

Despite wearing tie-up hiking shoes meant for hiking treacherous terrain, my unskilled feet slipped and struggled for a grip. I clung to the rope ladder and balanced myself with long chutes of bamboo that had probably been placed there for people like me who weren't practiced rope ladder climbers.

At the top, Dave led me along the river, hopping from rock to rock, most of them wet and slippery. I often felt unsteady and had to get down on all fours, sort of crawl-walking on my hands and feet, looking like an awkward humanoid arachnid. Sometimes the rocks were so difficult for me to navigate that I even scooted on my butt, not trusting myself on the stones.

Dave, on the other hand, hopped with ease from stone to stone. It was as if the stone reached out and grabbed his foot and pulled him into it. Energetically, it looked like in that moment, the energy of the stone reached halfway up Dave's calf, and for the moment that he put his full weight on the stone, his foot and leg and the stone became one energy, until the next stone reached up and grabbed Dave's other foot.

He didn't need to even really look where his feet were landing, he just hopped, with full faith, from step to step to step, trusting completely that he would be received by each stone, that it would support him fully.

I tried to follow his steps, placing my foot where his had just left, but it was like that little bit of effort, to watch and think where my foot would go in his place, was just enough willfulness to cancel out the energy of faith and surrender completely.

The whole trek for me was an effort, a challenge, a physical exertion that took all my focus and concentration. Where was my sukha, my surrender, my grace? In yoga I thought I had mastered the art of effort and grace balance, so why couldn't I apply it here on this river rock hopping?

When I teach yoga, I teach uddiyana bhanda, which literally translates to mean "upward lift lock." Physiologically, it is a subtle alignment and engagement of the psoas muscles and the diaphragm muscles in a sort of basket weave to support the core of the body from the inside. To align and hug those deep internal core muscles is to create a core stability that lifts the entire body and gives almost a floating sensation, especially during a yoga pose.

Emotionally, the uddiyana bhanda hugs the energy center of the body that governs one's sense of personal power, identity, strength, and independence. To hug those muscles has a confidence boosting effect because the movement literally makes you taller and makes you feel lighter and bigger.

However, if uddiyana is engaged too hard, the whole energy shifts to a sense of effort, losing sight of the surrender and grace of the pose. While following Dave, as much as I tried to use uddiyana to ease me through the hike, I couldn't surrender to the rocks. I couldn't find my faith. I couldn't trust myself.

So I asked Dave how he does it.

"You remember that Kahuna, the tribal elder I used to work with, Uncle Les?" One of the traits Dave had in common with bamboo was his deep respect for elders. Of all the grandchildren, Dave was the one of us who would to spend hours listening to the same stories of Grandpa's over and over again, long after the rest of us had found more interesting things to do.

"Yes."

"He prescribed for me to come hiking out here to claim my masculinity. Hiking these river rocks has taught me how to be a man."

"So what you're telling me is that, for me, it's hopeless because it's all about practice."

"Not at all. I was hiking river rocks for years, and was just as clumsy as you, before I got that prescription from Uncle Les. I was always hiking just to get to the waterfall, like you do. Looking for the pot of gold. But Uncle Les taught me to see it differently.

He told me to hike, not to get somewhere, but to remember something. He said that the bamboo that surrounds this river has a very masculine energy, and in some cultures, is even weapon-like. He suggested that I take a cue from the bamboo, in its ability to be very rooted and grow very tall. He told me to look at the bamboo as I hiked and claimed its energy in my mind as my own, the masculine that I am, I would remember how to be a man."

"I can see that you have become more manly since I was out here last," I said.

"Yeah, last time you were here, Angie and I were breaking up. I had that meeting with Uncle Les shortly after that. He told me I had an attraction to ambitious and independent women, and I had surrendered my manhood to serve their ambitions."

"I suppose that makes sense with Angie."

"And Celeste. And Jenn. Think about it, every woman I've been in relationship with was a strong and ambitious woman."

"I think maybe, big sister, you surrendered your femininity to Ted."

The truth hurts.

"It's true. You were the man in that relationship. You did everything from an active and masculine energy while he sat in meditation as a monk, a very feminine energy."

I slipped and landed my butt right in the river between two rocks.

"You know I'm right."

"Yeah," I surrendered, reaching my hand up to him, asking my very masculine baby brother to help me. "But how is the masculine bamboo supposed help me claim my femininity?"

"First of all, bamboo is not just masculine. It is the balance of yin and yang, just as much feminine as it is masculine. While it grows tall and fast like the masculine, it also has very feminine qualities like softness and pliability and flexibility."

"I get it. So how do I remember my femininity on this one hike, cuz I'm only here in Maui for a few days and don't have the opportunity to come here every day to practice?"

"You don't need practice. You just need a certain mindset. It has nothing to do with how you plant your foot or what you do with your body. It's a Jedi-mind trick."

"Great. Shall I just call you Yoda?"

"No, Uncle Les is the Yoda. Just call me Bro as you always do."

"Okay Bro-da, what's the secret to your Jedi-mind trick? Are you gonna tell me to use the force?"

"Listen, the feminine is about non-action, about taking the seed and letting it become what it is meant to become, nurturing it without controlling it. You gotta let go of control."

"How do I do that?"

"Look up."

"What?"

"When you step, don't look where your foot is going, look up ahead of you."

"Seriously? That sounds so, well, simple. But at the same time, so HARD."

"Trust me. You look up ahead at the path in front of you. Your brain is smart enough to survey the scene and figure out the best path without your consciousness having to get involved.

"It's like your eyes receive the path, including all the possible pitfalls, and your subconscious mind maps out the best course for you and sends the message to your feet. Your conscious brain never has to think about where to step. That's the feminine. Letting the parts of you do what they're meant to do, and taking the action out of the parts that don't need to be 'doing.' That way your conscious brain can focus on other things."

"Like what?" I asked.

"Like listening to your really smart baby brother tell you stories."

"Okay. Hold on. Give me a sec to think about this."

"That's just it, Sis. You CAN'T think about it. You just gotta go with it."

He grabbed my hand and pulled me, his grip so strong that I didn't have a choice to let go if I wanted to. He was standing in his masculine, showing me the way, with a penetrating force. At first I felt like a ragdoll being dragged behind, my feet and ankles getting occasionally stuck on and between the stones. I thought I would be completely bruised by the time we got to the waterfall. I kept watching my feet, and with every other step, I stumbled.

"Look up!" He instructed as he pulled a little harder on my wrist. When I did, even though he had told me what would happen, I was shocked. As I looked ahead at the rocks, my feet just sort of scurried underneath me.

I hopped and climbed from stone to stone as if I had hiked this gorge many times before. I scaled the tall boulders and scurried across the flat rocks, and even allowed myself to splash into a shallow puddle when my feet decided it was the most stable option.

"It worked," Dave said.
"Shhh. Don't jinx it."
"We're there."
"Where?"
"To the part where we stop scaling river rocks and we swim."
"Swim?"

"Yep. See?" He pointed to a tree where some other hikers had left their clothes and pulled of his t-shirt. He threw his slippahs into a deep channel and jumped in to retrieve them as they floated across the surface with the current. I stripped down to my bikini, leaving my hiking shoes on, I took the leap behind him.

"I wish I'd worn my flip-flops. Swimming in hiking shoes is not fun."

"That's a whole other lesson," Dave laughed.

After a short swim we came across the most glorious waterfall I had ever seen. The water plummeted from high above into a deep pool of shiny blue-green water. The bright green algae and greenery surrounding the waterfall contrasted perfectly with the blue water.

Millions of tiny little leaves caught the light of the sun and reflected diamond facets into the pool. The pool was a bed of smoothed river stones carved into a perfect womb. The water splashed off the pool and bounced up into the leaves, sending shimmers of light in little tiny prisms absolutely everywhere.

"My dear sister, this is the feminine."

"Look at her power!" I exclaimed.

I floated in the pool, the splash of the waterfall misting my face as I drank in the contrast of the warm sun and the cool water on my skin. My bandages almost gone, my scars exposed, I felt free.

A Soul Cleansing

*"The old has passed away;
behold, the new has come."*
~2 Corinthians 5:17

My brother's neighbors invited me on a walk, down the hill from Dave's house through some fields to a sacred bay. It was a rocky beach with rough waters splashing into several crystal clear tide pools protected by reefs and rocks.

Something about this bay, in all its tropical beauty, was very sad. Perhaps the sadness I felt was my own. Just before the hike, Julie had called to tell me that she and Tim had to put Millie down the day before. She was 14 years old, ancient for a black lab, and she had cancer.

They had hoped she wouldn't succumb to the worst symptoms until after they returned to Minnesota for the spring and summer, but were happy that at least she made it to receive her Animal Companion of the Year Award from the Minnesota Veterinary Association.

I cried halfway down the gorge to the bay as I thought about how Millie and her lab-lean had healed me when she was suffering in her own way. But the sadness I felt once I got to the bay was heavier than just my grief for Millie's death.

The color of the water at the rim of the shore reminded me of the iciness of Ted's eyes, and my newly exposed scars ached like the phantom pain of an amputated limb. I felt the familiar silk knot between my shoulder blades tighten.

While my companions explored the rocky shore, I told them that I had just got news that a friend's dog died, and I sat on a rock and looked at pictures of Millie on my phone. I recognized the pressure of Grief's squeeze on various parts of my body, but this time, instead of resisting, I surrendered to his pressure, and it felt almost like a nice hug as I let the tears spill down my face.

I cried for Millie. I cried for Julie and Tim. And in time, I knew I was crying for myself as well. While I was no longer crying for the loss of my marriage, I had new layers to grieve. To me, a dog's greeting, like Millie, is directly connected to the warmth of home.

The loss of Millie triggered in me grief for the loss of my home. After spending a week watching homeless hippies living in tents wandering the streets and shores of Pa'ia, my own homelessness had become all too apparent to me.

While the hippies had chosen their plight for the most part, happy to hitchhike from beach to beach and beg for odd jobs for food, I had been turned out from the home I had built with Ted. I wasn't quite as homeless as a hippie in that I never had to worry about a bed to sleep in, a bathroom to use, or a kitchen to prepare my meals.

I had plenty of homes to welcome me, but I didn't have my own home. A heavy wave left a mist on my face, and the salty speckles seemed to pull the tears out of my eyes. There was something about this bay, an energy that pulled the pain out from under the surface.

My sobs were thicker than I had ever felt before, and I knew the sadness in this space was heavier than what I could have carried down the gorge myself. I recognized the sadness, the heavy depression, but it was denser than I had ever felt before, and the density seemed to be from deep underneath my roots. Like it was dredging up grievances from my great-great grandmothers that resided in my blood.

The bay was full of centuries worth of tears. The crash of the water on the rocks carried the echoes of sadness from every person who has ever visited this bay, not to mention the residue of ancestral sadness coded into their bones.

The stones of Hawaii, particularly this bay, are the sponges that absorb the legends of the people who come to Hawaii and bathe on her shores. They absorb the stories, the history, the pains, the sadness, the heaviness, the burdens, the labor, the betrayal, and the aches, as well as the joys, pleasures, births, and rejoicing.

Each stone is a piece of our collective history, as well as a necessary organ of Pele's being. They speak to each other through the crash of the waves and echo the stories of history forever. The stones are her memory keepers. Legend says that Pele spares none of her wrath on those who take her stones from her.

It is said that if some unsuspecting soul takes a stone from Hawaii, he is destined to a life of bad luck and turmoil until the stone is returned to the home from which it was found. When one is taken, the frequency must travel through the bones of the person who took it to connect back to its source, ricocheting the turmoil of all the sadness gathered into her history through the being of the ignorant soul who took a piece of her as a souvenir.

This bay attracts and extracts the heaviest burdens and the most grotesque sorrows of life so that Pele, the goddess of Hawaii, may smooth and ease the pain by eroding the sharpest of it with her saltwater tears. Hawaii holds these sadnesses in her womb, and as more and more tourists discover the magic of her healing, the deeper her sadness resounds. Through Dave's stories and perspective, I had witnessed dozens of sadnesses and injustices that Maui has suffered at the hands of ignorant haoles--non-natives on Maui--and didn't necessarily value or respect the indigenous traditions.

A colleague of Dave's tells a story of visiting this bay as a young child with his uncle in the 1950s. On more than one occasion, they would encounter an ugly scene. Men would string a cable from one end of the bay to the other. They would shoot a dog on the beach, and string the carnage onto the cable to drip blood into the bay and attract sharks, which they would then shoot with rifles as well.

Over half a century later, the cliffs above the bay is now often home to individuals addicted to ice, the Hawaiian version of crystal meth, a drug that brings out the ugliest of behaviors from the deepest shadows of the human soul. Having witnessed a couple of junkies shooting up in a parking lot behind a realtor's office just a few days earlier, I imagine my feelings at that moment were very similar to Dave's colleague stumbling upon the brutal murder of dogs and sharks. I'd never witnessed illegal drug use, other than in the movies, and I felt a bit like a child walking into a scene that was way beyond my comprehension. Their energy was completely manic, frenetic, like bugs were crawling under their skin in some kind of paranormal horror film.

Just on the other side of the bay are a number of birthing pools, protected by a reef and a small stream. In ancient times, indigenous Hawaiian women in labor would hike down treacherous cliffs to these pools to give birth, offering the pains of their childbirth to be softened by the sweetness of Pele's nectar. These women literally sat in one of Pele's thousands of wombs to give birth and allow their babes to be washed of the harshest pains of birth as they were received into the earthly world.

In that moment, holding hands with both Grief and Joy, I felt like I was in labor, having spent the last couple months in a long slow death of my life, I was about to give birth to myself.

I imagine that to the stones of this bay, the vibrations of the wails of mothers in labor and cries of newborn infants in the birthing pools are virtually indiscernible from the yelps of the dying dogs or the mad shrieks of ice addicts. The veil between dichotomies is thin.

Death and birth dance the boundary between heaven and earth, twirling around each other like the swirling waters in the tide pools. The ugly pain and decay of death provides nourishment for the beautiful pleasure of birth, a resurrection. Was it no accident that I found my way here on Maundy Thursday, just a few days before the celebration of the resurrection of Christ?

We skipped across the boulders and climbed along the cliff to the tide pools. As I watched my companions swim in the pools, I saw the subtlest of their pains evaporate off their skin, absorbed by the warm rays of the sun. I envied them. I wanted to dig inside myself, to bring my sadness to the surface so it could be rinsed away in the frothy surf.

For my entire stay in Maui, every time I had the opportunity to swim, I dreaded the cold water, resistant to the salty sting on my wounds. At this sacred bay, however, I yearned for the cold water. I craved the sting. Perhaps what I really wanted was the smoothness that comes after the sting. But alas, I didn't have a swimming suit, nor the courage to go naked with my brother's neighbors just a few feet away. I wandered over to a pool on the other side of the reef, where Grief stood hand in hand with Joy.

They reached out to me, and I welcomed their invitation. Grief's cold and knotty fingers laced my left hand while Joy's warm and soft skin embraced my right hand. I could only know the full sweetness of Joy in contrast to the sharp stabs of Grief. A smooth stone is only smooth in relation to one with sharp edges. There on that beach, my emotions collectively gathered underneath my feet. Sadness and loneliness braced up against happiness and peace, and sometimes wedged underneath joy and calm.

I took off my shoes and socks, sat on a boulder, and wedged my feet and toes between the stones. I closed my eyes, felt the stones and water on my feet, and breathed as deeply as I could. Just as water finds the deepest buried stone and smoothes it over time; my breath reached the deepest pains inside me and soothed them.

One of the indigenous aunties who taught Dave Hawaiian spirituality describes the human soul as an empty bowl, that holds only light, like the bowl of a bay. The water of the bay reflects the light of the sun, revealing the true essence of nature.

The stones, shells, driftwood and debris in the bay are symbolic of all the experiences and stories and history of our lives that block the light. I wanted to dig down beneath the surface of the debris of my life and find the light of my empty bowl underneath.

The indigenous Hawaiians use an o'o (pronounced oh-oh), a long stick or staff, to dig and bury. The action of lifting and pushing the o'o into the ground, the moment of penetration and retraction, a very sexual masculine action, is symbolic of accessing depth in life, connecting to the bone depth of Source.

To dig or penetrate the earth with an o'o is to connect to the wisdom of Mother Earth and to call upon the guidance of the ancestors who have been buried in her. I wanted to use my whole body as an o'o to get to the Source.

The pinch of the rocks on the pads of my toes felt comforting, like the stones could squeeze the juice out my pores. If I could only dig deeper, I might be able to access all the wisdom of my ancestry, coded in the DNA of my blood and bones, bring it to the surface so that I might then rinse away the harshest pieces of it in the salty waters of the tide pools.

When the stones bit my pinky toe, reminiscent of the bitter wind at the north woods Minnesota cabin where I had my grief ritual, I recognized the chill of Grief under my skin, and I greeted him with a melancholy smile. I felt sorrow ooze through the nerve endings of my feet and asked Grief to inject them into the stones to become part of the cacophony of sound that echoes among the walls of this sacred bay. The sun beat hot on my skin, and my pores cried salty sweat tears. Each bite of a stone was like a stitch of my wounds coming out. As my body cried, my face and heart rejoiced in the dichotomy of destruction and creation, birth and death, pleasure and pain.

When the chill under my skin subsided, I removed my feet from the stones. Unable to walk, I could only imagine that the intensity of the pain I felt was a fraction of what it was like to give birth.

Had I just given birth to myself, my soul? I scooted my seat from rock to rock until I reached the nearest pool a few feet away, and dangled my soles into her clear water. The nectar of Pele's womb lapped at my arches and the salt exfoliated the calluses of my heels. My feet absorbed the glittery sand bottom of the pool, and for just a moment I thought that the soles of my feet were windows to my soul. The vibration of the two worlds, identical as the wails of newborn babes and dying pups.

I've heard that mothers forget the pain of childbirth as soon as the babe is laid in her arms. I wouldn't know, but the pain of my wounds was now gone as I looked at the birth of my new life and my true self in the reflection of the water. At that moment, as I felt myself resurrected through baptism, I felt more alive than I could ever remember, like I was breathing in the vitality of experience through the pores of my skin.

On the walk back to Dave's house, I passed a young couple with a small child in a red wagon, the kind with the slatted wood siding. The child couldn't have been more than a year old, and she had her hands on the lip of each edge. She sat upright on a blanket, her eyes and energy acutely alert to take in the fullness of her surroundings. In walking behind this wagon, I had a very vivid memory of being that child, riding in the wagon that my mother pulled.

I could feel the slates on the palms of my hands and the rumble of the pavement under my legs. I could smell my own sweat under my sun hat, and feel the texture of the blanket, slightly moist from my perspiration, under my thighs. It was a very small moment, but very significant for me to remember what it felt like to be that child, sitting upright and alert, aware of the world around me in all its newness.

It was a beautiful moment, tapping into the memory in the recess of my brain that goes back further than any conscious memory I've ever had. There was a sweetness to remembering that innocence, that openness, that full-on awareness of everything about my experience.

That night, a lead story on the news was of Pope Francis, breaking tradition to wash the feet of a female Muslim prisoner on Maundy Thursday. I received my own soul cleansing from Pele that day.

Teri Leigh

Loving the Scars ~ Celebrating Success

Rainbow Eucalyptus Scars

"'Who are you?' asked the Caterpillar.
'I hardly know, Sir. I know who I was,
but I think I must have changed."
~Alice's Adventures in Wonderland, Lewis Carroll

After my rebirthing at the sacred bay, my bandages removed, my stitches pulled out. My wounds were now sealed, formed into a solid, yet protective scar tissue. Although the scars were not pretty, and occasionally, if hit just the right way, they would cause a shudder of pain through me, but they no longer defined my experience or consumed my being. At the same time, I was able to recognize that someday, very soon, I might be able to touch those scars lovingly and tell the story of their inception.

I was no longer hurting about letting go of Ted, or my home, or the dreams I had for my marriage and my future. The parts of those fears and anxieties and pains that couldn't be washed away by Pele were sealed underneath the scar. I no longer felt cold by the emptiness inside me. Instead, I felt a great sense of expansion.

I had also found a way of understanding that sadness and grief, although consuming emotions, are not defining emotions. It is so easy to confuse my emotions with my identity, but in making myself into the o'o I learned how to feel grief and sadness and not let it define me.

My sadness didn't have to define me anymore than the etchings of "Johnny loves Debbie" define the rainbow eucalyptus trees on the side of Hana Highway.

The rainbow eucalyptus grove is one of my favorite places to visit on Maui. Walking through the grove is like walking through a wonderland. The trees have multi-colored trunks that ooze oil spill tears of greens and oranges and yellows and pinks down their faces.

A simple foot-trodden path between them has been worn by thousands of tourists taking in the magic of these beings. As I had learned, almost everything of beauty in Maui had been tainted by tourisms scars, but the scars didn't define the magic of the island, nonetheless.

I wanted to visit each one of the dozen trees, and hug each one, to apologize for the transgressions of my fellow human beings. I felt compassion well up inside me as I embraced each tree that had been tattooed with jagged lacerations of messages similar to what is written on the bathroom stalls at gas stations.

With each embrace of each tree, I felt an overwhelming sense of sweetness, and generosity, and nurturing, as if I could sense that the tree was actually happy to sacrifice a piece of itself for each of the carvings in trade for the spark happiness of the individual leaving the mark. Nature always provides. These trees will always provide smiles and joys to tourists, just like the sun will always provide light to those in the dark, and the ocean will never dry up or withhold its salt to those who need to be washed and healed.

There were so many hidden sadnesses of Maui, like the scarred eucalyptus trees. In my short two weeks on the island, Dave had told me a multitude of stories about the beauties of the island being eroded and corrupted. Whether it was landowners running locals out of business for higher property values, or big business wanting to take over a sacred harbor to park their Super Ferry, or white hippies taking advantage of lenient welfare laws originally put in place to compensate and support the native communities, the sad stories rarely had a happy ending. Yet, Pele continues to provide, to heal and wash and nurture everyone who steps on her shores.

Every day on the drive into Pa'ia, we passed the boarded up Kuau Mart that used to be run by the native Aunties. These elders would serve the locals from their own homegrown gardens, the produce being grown with love and selfless service. But one day, the rich white landowner decided he could put a business in place of the

The Gift Inside the Wound

Kuau Mart that would raise his property value and attract more tourists than locals. He jacked up the Aunties rent over 150 percent and demanded 10 percent of their profits until they were forced into retirement, a term the Aunties didn't understand. The new renter backed out on the lease under intimidation of the locals threat to run them out of business by boycott, vandalism, arson, or worse. The Kuau Mart remains boarded up and empty, the dual between the landlord and the locals at a standstill. Over time, the locals have built a fence of surfboards along the side of the mart. Dave made a surfboard for the fence, writing an epithet on it in honor of the aunties.

As always, within a day of a message being left for the Aunties at the Mart, the landlord painted over my brother's loving gesture, leaving a black blob where his message had been. That night, with a headlamp and a razor blade, Dave scraped the paint off, and his epithet remains untouched today.

While most stories ended sadly like Kuau Mart, occasionally the native Hawaiians were able to work the system and maintain one of their sacred spaces. Kahului Harbor houses a body-boarding wave that is favored among the poor native children who live in the nearby ghettos.

A few years back the tourism industry wanted to bring the SuperFerry into the harbor, eliminating the natives last healthy form of entertainment. When the city council convened to vote on the SuperFerry, the meeting was flooded with local culture.

The meeting went on for hours as dozens of community members spoke for their allotted three minutes in defense of keeping the harbor ferry free.

When renowned and respected elder Uncle Les rose to speak, he ignored all warnings of his time limit and continued talking well after his three minutes. The timekeeper repeatedly tried to interrupt him until finally one of the natives served as Uncle Les' bodyguard got up and said in a stern and unquestionable voice, "Don't disrespect your elder. Uncle Les is speaking. You listen."

Later, a famous native surfer who had made a name for himself internationally, gave his three minutes as a simple testimonial. He stood up powerfully and pounded his chest like a gorilla. "You see this body. You know what it can do. This harbor built this body. It made me."

His testimonial along with the vibrations of the voice of Uncle Les put a hypnotizing charm on the city council, or perhaps they feared the silent argument that would continue if they didn't surrender, and they voted to save the harbor from the Super Ferry.

There's a joke that when the white man came to the islands, he told the natives to put clothes on because being naked was savage. And now, the natives roll their eyes at the white man's desire to be naked on the island.

For decades, haoles have been trying to adulterate the island of Maui with their property values and other money-making ventures. And while Pele, like Mother Earth, doesn't reject her children, even the ones who try to capitalize on her generosity, She never ever loses sight of her identity, her own nakedness, and her purpose.

I was a haole, a white woman from suburbia who had come to the island wrapped heavily in the bandages of my wounds, and Pele helped me to remove those bandages and look at my own nakedness.

On my last day on Maui, I ventured into a small cove between Pa'ia Beach and Baldwin Beach. I stripped naked and stood at the edge of the shoreline staring out at the vast sea. The feeling wasn't unlike the feeling I had looking out the window of the airplane and reading "do not step outside this area" on the wing.

There was a vast emptiness, but thanks to the skilled mothering I had received along my journey, sealed finally by the divine mothering of Pele, that emptiness now looked like a vast openness of possibilities.

"Who am I? I hardly know." I felt like Alice in Wonderland talking to the caterpillar smoking a hookah on a mushroom. The world I had known was no longer real, and the world I was dancing in felt surreal.

I didn't want to end up like the Auntie who drove by the Kuau Mart every day, unsure of what to do with herself. I didn't want to be like the naked old man on Little Beach, wearing just a watch, chasing money and controlled by time. I didn't want to turn out like the Maui hippies, a welfare bum, just living off the goodwill of my friends.

No.

I wanted to stand up in front of a large crowd of people, pound my chest like a gorilla and say out loud, "You see this woman who stands in front of you. She is the Divine Feminine. My wounds MADE me."

Yet I still didn't know what they made. I knew what I didn't want to be and what I didn't want to do. In terms of what I did want, well, I had only the vague impressions left by the panther. As for the rest, I was excited to find out. And, I wasn't afraid anymore about being naked in the process. I'd come to Maui battered and bandaged, in a major state of identity crisis. I was leaving Maui, bandages removed, raw and vulnerable, but strong.

I was getting ready to leave Maui changed, but not changed. I realized that I didn't know who I was, but that I didn't want to define myself by external factors anymore. My home, my husband, and my marriage were things I had wrapped around myself, to cover and protect the soft vulnerability underneath.

It was time to go, to show my scars and tell the stories that made them.

When I hugged Dave goodbye, I felt like Alice in Wonderland waking up on the riverbank next to a scarred rainbow eucalyptus tree after a long and confusing dream.

Wonder Twin Powers – ACTIVATE!

"Bro, I think I'm gonna change my name."
"To what?"
"Teri Alice Leigh."
"Alice, like Grandma, dad's mom?"
"Yeah…and like Alice…in Wonderland," I said.
"I like it," he kissed the top of my head, his blessing.

Teri Leigh

The Gift Inside the Wound

Objects in Mirror Are Closer Than They Appear

"It's good to glance at the rearview mirror to see how far you've come, but if you stare too long, you'll miss what's right in front of you."
~Author Unknown

After I got back to the mainland, I reunited with Ted to finalize the details of our divorce. On the way to the restaurant, Ted drove as I stared out the passenger sideview mirror. He felt so far away, so small, like the yellow mini Cooper behind us and one lane over. But, Fuck You Sunday was just a few months ago, and he was sitting right next to me.

My past was not that far behind me, yet I still felt like I needed to check in with it before changing lanes on my journey. I knew I couldn't trust the image I saw in the mirror. I knew I had to turn my body and look over my shoulder before making a move that would put him directly behind me. I wasn't yet ready to change lanes entirely even though he was well behind me waving me over.

He drank tea while I sipped wine over polite conversation. I told him the more benign stories from my travels. He told me about a couple movies he had watched. By the time our appetizers arrived, the conversation naturally turned to the final divorce negotiations. It was easier, perhaps safer, to have this discussion in public than back at the house.

Grief squeezed my hand again. Strength showed herself standing next to Grief. Ted waved me to drive in front of him, leave him in the house, leave him in our old life, to move forward on the road, on my own.

Yet, I wasn't ready to change lanes, afraid that if I did, he would turn off the road altogether when I wasn't looking. What I recognized in that moment, in the blankness of his emotions and the fullness of my own, he hadn't ever really been in the same car with me. Ever.

That made me cry.

I wept openly there in the restaurant, big silent wet glistening tears. No sobs, just wetness.

"I know this probably sounds really strange given the circumstances," he continued, "but you look radiantly beautiful right now."

It was perhaps the first genuine compliment he had given me in years. Oddly, I understood exactly what he meant. As I wept, I stepped outside of myself. The sequins and rhinestones of my shawl caught the light in the glistening wetness of my tears.

"Yes. Thank you."

Over papadam and samosas, Ted explained that he had retained a lawyer, solely to draw up the paperwork based on what we decided together. He spent the entire entrée course listing things we had in the house that he thought were valuable that I should have. He explained what his lawyer said was standard practice in terms of splitting debts and pensions and IRAs. I nodded in agreement and let the water spill from my eyes.

He offered to watch Sukha for me while I took my next trip to Cleveland. He would have the final divorce papers drawn up for me to sign when I came back to retrieve Sukha at the end of May. He suggested I make arrangements then to come and pack up whatever I wanted because he didn't care much about "stuff." I just nodded and let the wetness drip into my basmati rice.

He paid the bill, and we went home.

That night, when I climbed into our marital bed for the last time, Ted came up to the bedroom as if to tuck me in. He watched me snuggle with Sukha under the covers and set the alarm for me. Then he went downstairs to read. He crawled into bed a few hours later, and kissed me on the forehead. I rolled over and let my tears wet the pillow with my back to him.

The next morning, he helped pack my car. When he shut the back-hatch-door, he turned and looked me in the eye. I felt his whole being through his soft blue eyes. It was as if his essence grew fingers through the flecks of his irises and reached down through the specks of gold in my eyes and massaged my heart from the inside. Then he hugged me, and didn't let go. I felt like he was massaging every red blood cell in my entire body.

Then he kissed me. It was a kiss exactly like our very first kiss.

His lips soft and sweet, supple and gentle, blended with mine where I couldn't feel where his ended and mine began. It wasn't a kiss of passion or desire. It wasn't a kiss of nurturing or need. It wasn't a kiss of expression.

It was a kiss of existence.

Love is a state of being.

I felt the vibration of it like a soft oboe playing the initial tuning note for the orchestra and every instrument of my body to the tune of our lips, remembering its perfect pitch in harmony and melody with everything else in the universe.

Time and space no longer existed. We weren't in our garage in January 2013, or the parking lot of the yoga studio where we shared our first kiss in December 2001. We were in both places at the same time, and all the space in between, squished together into this one moment, encompassing our entire relationship.

While at the same time, that one kiss took me back 11 years to realize that time and emotions are completely incongruous and irrelevant. Eleven years of building resentments and annoyances and stories and history evaporated, completely erased as we reached inside ourselves and just touched the button. Hidden and lost in our hearts, the button said, "this is who you are together."

Ta-da for that one moment of that one kiss, everything of time and space and separateness and disagreement…disintegrated.

We were one.
My pain was his pain.
My sadness was his sadness.
My love was his love.

I eventually pulled away, hitting the restart button back on Time. He walked me to the driver's side door, reluctant to let go.

"Let me know that you get there okay," he said. I nodded and climbed into the car.

Where?
Where am I going?
Where is home?
There is no Destination...there is no place.

In his goodbye kiss, Ted gave me a gift to carry with me on my journey. This gift wasn't intended to provide me hope that I could one day return to him and renew this feeling, but was more an affirmation, a recognition that this piece of me exists inside of me, and I can take it with me wherever I go.

And so, I set out for Cleveland. And the rumble of the road underneath me stirred up all my emotions. Grief settled down in the passenger seat, and all his friends piled into the back seat. I put my hand on the gear shift, and his bony cold hand on top of it.

Grief comes in waves, and never really goes away.

At first, for a fleeting moment, I felt Peace. Her hand on my shoulder. I settled into a space of re-living his kiss on my lips and enjoying the space it provided for us both to explore the world in new ways, together on a spiritual realm albeit separate in physical space.

Then I'd focus on the sensation he'd left on my lips and Hope tapped her thumbs on my heart like a drum. The syncopated rhythm she tapped was familiar, patterns and thoughts that quickly sent my mind buzzing. Maybe this is just a temporary separation, and when I get back, having spent some time with myself and he having spent some time with himself, we can figure out a better way to be together. He always had been the love of my life. Ted was IT for me. Attachment shoved Hope out the window. He brought Yearning and Obsession with him. They flapped their wings around the confined space of my mind, and car for several miles.

But Grief wouldn't let them stay for long. With the lift of one finger, Grief, summoned Sadness and Loneliness out from under the floor mats.

I miss the Ted I married.

The Gift Inside the Wound

But why would I miss the man who didn't love himself?

Grief opened the window a crack, and Pity flew in. For every compliment he had ever denied, for the years and years I'd watch him abuse his body with excessive and extreme exercise, for the deprivation I had witnessed in his eating disordered behaviors that drove me crazy. For 10 years he had loved me and supported me and not loved himself.

Pity morphed to Guilt. Was it my fault? Did I use up all the love he had and take all the love he had for himself on me? Did I drain his supply and was now leaving him with nothing?

Guilt vacillated with Resentment like a teeter totter. As much as he said he loved me, he had neglected me. He was an asshole. Or was he an asshole because I was needy?

Maybe he had nothing left to give because I had sucked him dry so now I had to leave so he could replenish himself. Or was he just a selfish bastard whose mother spoiled him as an only child and he only knew how to put his own pursuits above everyone else, even my health? Perhaps it was both, he's a selfish bastard because I drained him, AND I was needy because he was a selfish bastard.

As I drove on that long stretch of interstate from Minnesota to Ohio, I looked in my rear view mirrors, all three of them, and saw wide open empty highway.

My car was full with all kinds of Grief's friends, my demons. But Ted. Ted was no longer behind me, next to me, or even inside the car with me. Instead, he lingered on the dendrites and neurons of my memories.

The images that appeared in my mirrors, and the view through my back windshield... they all lived in history, and story, and time and space. What lived beyond time and space, beyond the reflection of the mirrors was the energy inside that kiss, a reminder that underneath all the drama and the chaos, behind the veils of the emotions and the impermanence was the one constant.

Love.

Love, Ted's final gift to me, lingered on my lips from his kiss, not as a memory, but as a button in the heart in my being.

Teri Leigh

Bless Me, Saturday

> *"Generally, by the time you are Real,*
> *most of your hair has been loved off,*
> *and your eyes drop out*
> *and you get loose in the joints and very shabby.*
> *But these things don't matter at all,*
> *because once you are Real you can't be ugly,*
> *except to people who don't understand."*
>
> ~Margery Williams <u>The Velveteen Rabbit</u>

In Cleveland, I checked into a small spiritual center that was home to a number of darling sweet nuns. Usually when I teach at a studio, the studio owner puts me up in her guest bedroom, or couch, or I crash in my sleeping bag on her living room floor. But the studio owner in Cleveland suggested I might enjoy this spiritual center more than the chaos of her home. I agreed, especially when she said she had cats. How appropriate that Fuck You Sunday was Ted's desire to live a monk-life, and here I was, living for the weekend with nuns, just days after agreeing to divorce terms and awaiting the paperwork to sign.

Each morning and night I took my journal with me to the dining hall and wrote as I ate and listened to the conversations of the sweet nuns at the next table. By Saturday dinner, I felt like I knew these tender women through their stories and affections to each other, all while remaining rather invisible myself.

Or so I thought.

"Excuse me," Sister Juanita tapped me on the shoulder. She was the only African American of the bunch, a tiny postage stamp of a woman who couldn't have been more than four-foot-nine and total of 95 pounds. She was also my favorite. I swear she wore a pink halo that kissed the forehead of everyone she greeted with her gentle smile and soft eyes. She didn't just walk into a room, she floated, like a wispy feather dusting the floor behind her.

"Pardon me, am I in your way?" Self-conscious of my body odor, I backed a step away from her. I had just come from teaching back-to-back workshops in a hot yoga room. My hair was tied up in a frizzy knot on top of my head, and my clothes were still slightly damp from sweat.

"No, my dear," she stepped closer, closing the gap I had just created, so as to rest her hand on my shoulder. The warmth of her hand radiated into me. I felt as though she were purposely blessing me with her touch, as the minister did for me in Lutheran Communion when I was a child.

"I just wanted to tell you that you are radiantly beautiful. Did you just walk off a runway? You are absolutely stunning."

Her touch melted into me as if she were massaging my scars, musing about the beauty they had tattooed on my soul.

I was speechless. In just three sentences, this tiny woman somehow grew to 10-feet tall and sprouted 20- foot wings out of her shoulder blades. Her wings wrapped around me in the soft embrace of her words. The feathers of her wings dusted away any insecurities and anxieties I had ever had. The warmth of her pink aura snuggled itself under the top layers of my skin. I just stood there for a moment and gazed into her eyes receiving her blessing.

Yes, Thank You.

"Thank you. I just walked off a yoga mat," I stammered.

"Well, my sweets, it works for you. Thank you for gracing me with your energy today," Sister Juanita gave my shoulder a little squeeze, and as gracefully as she appeared, she floated away.

When I got back to my room, I went into the bathroom for a shower. I stood in front of the mirror, completely naked, and stared at myself for a good long time, looking for what Sister Juanita had seen.

The Gift Inside the Wound

Having lost about 10 pounds on "the divorce diet" my skin was loose on my bones, especially through my eyes and cheeks, leaving a tired expression. My body was showing all the signs of almost 40 years of resisting gravity. For the first time in my life, as I looked at myself, I felt old. I pushed my palms into my closed eyes and rubbed hard. And then, I leaned into the mirror and pulled at the skin on my face, tugging at my eyes and cheeks.

Then I climbed up and sat on the vanity, my feet in the sink, so I could get my face right up next to the mirror, and I looked into my own eyes. I sat there and stared until my vision completely blurred. Through distorted vision, I saw myself as wrinkled and withered. The folds around my eyes deepened. The browns of my eyes got darker, almost black, like soil.

I saw myself as an old woman.

I wondered how old Sister Juanita was. She was somehow ageless. She could have been 50 or 90. It didn't seem to matter. All that mattered was how her light filled the large cafeteria, as she had told me mine did.

I focused on the darkness and emptiness of the pupil of my right eye. My brown irises blended with the blackness. The deeper I looked into the darkness, the more I saw my wounds and the wrinkles and scars weathered by those wounds.

Then, finally, I saw what Sister Juanita saw.

Rays of light pierced through the wrinkles of my scars. The image was absolutely beautiful, like sun beams pouring from the cracks of my eyes, multi-colored, multi-faceted, brilliant and iridescent. My eyes filled with tears, and the tears refracted the light into thousands of prisms of color, everywhere.

The wound is where the light of your gift comes out of you.

~TeriLeigh

Teri Leigh

Blessing

May you find yourself at home in your body and your being
For Home is not a place, but a feeling.

May you find love in your spirit and soul.
For Love is not an emotion, but a state of being.

May you find yourself tenderly wounded from time to time,
For a Wound is not a curse, but a Precious Gift.

Exactly four years after Fuck You Sunday, to the day, in the dead of Minnesota winter, I found myself unexpectedly "homeless" and single, once again. This time, I knew I wasn't *really* homeless. In fact, because I had a team of angels waiting to receive me, I knew I was homeFULL. This time, I had new legs, and wings, stronger ones. This time, there was no gash in my earth to fall into. Rather, I made the conscious decision to flip every apparent negative on its head or turn it inside out to find the gift inside the wound.

When the door of the house where I was living closed and locked behind me unexpectedly that bitter winter Minnesota day, Fear and Anxiety waited on the curb. But, Fear quickly shed his parka and showed his true identity to be Excitement. Anxiety took off his ski mask and his scowl turned to a smile, shape-shifting him into Anticipation. They took my hands and led me to my car, inviting me back on the road.

How could I refuse!?

When I snapped on my seatbelt, Loneliness RSVPd her regrets and sent her twin sister Solitude to be my companion. Laughter met me under the waterfalls of Maui, while Tears took her vacation somewhere else, far away. Peace joined me on the icy Illinois interstate. She was invited by Chaos who had a last-minute emergency, so he couldn't attend. Passion led my way through Kentucky and Tennessee. She stole her invitation from her cousin Anger, who stayed home to stir his stew. Joy met me under the warm sunshine of Florida, but left her brother Sorrow at home.

Ten weeks later Grief welcomed me into his arms in the mountains of New Mexico when I set to the task of editing this book for publication. We greeted like old friends. He removed his hooded cape, bearing his heart to me, revealing himself as Love.

THE TEACHING

Teri Leigh

Finding the Gifts Inside Your Own Wounds

The Gift Inside the Wound
A Letter to My Readers

"Your heart and my heart are very old friends."

~Hafiz

Dear Reader,

As I wrote this book, when I finished the last page and submitted the PDF files to the printers, I couldn't just close my laptop and pat myself on the back for a job well done. I couldn't say goodbye to you, my reader, that easily. Whenever I get to the end of reading a good book, I always feel sadness. The characters have become my new best friends, and closing the book feels like saying goodbye to them, not knowing if I'll ever see them again. I have a hard time closing the back cover for the last time because I don't want my friends to get smooshed by the pages or disappear into the binding.

My work here has only just begun.

As much as I am a writer, I am also a teacher. My teaching comes from the threaded fabric of my stories, like the morals attached to Aesop's fables and Grimm's fairy tales. As your storyteller, I hope that my stories prove to you that inside every painful wound is a precious gift to be cherished. As your teacher, I hope you will allow me to show you the more specific lessons I learned along the way, guide you through your own healing process, and offer you insights, strategies, and tools to heal your own wounds and find the gifts inside them.

I want to spend more time with you and give you more opportunities to spend more time with me, and not just as a writer and a reader, but as a teacher and a student, as travel companions. I want to invite you on a road trip. So please, climb in the backseat of my car, let me show you what comes next.

What comes next is more exciting to me than anything that this book has already given you. I want to show you HOW I followed the threads of stress tangled inside my nervous system and discovered specific strategies to tame the mental monsters trying to play a game of cat and mouse with my emotions. I want to give you the step-by-step instruction on specific strategies, simple daily exercises that I used to turn the coins of negativity upside down to discover Courage inside Fear, Empathy inside Guilt, Solitude inside Loneliness, Strength inside Vulnerability, and Passion inside Anger.

Please join me at Mindfulness Online Academy for a continuation of this journey. I offer one-on-one coaching and a variety of online courses, including divorce coaching and mindfulness courses based on this book.

Teri Leigh

www.MindfulnessOnlineAcademy.com
www.TeriLeigh.com

The Gift Inside the Wound

Acknowledgements

Gratitude is an open door to abundance.

When I reflect on being a wandering nomad traveller healing from the deepest gashes in my emotional being, I am consumed with gratitude for the many souls and spirits who aided in my healing and supported me through this process.

Neil Cunningham, your humble Hobbit presence in my life has left invisible ink fingerprints in the spaces between words and in the silences between the beats of my heart. Thank you for knowing me, hearing and feeling the vibrations of my voice and helping to tap the rhythm and cadence of my truths onto these pages with your gentle nudges and carefully crafted subtle change suggestions. Thank you for holding me up, keeping me humble, and of course making me laugh every single day.

Megan Punt, my wandering spirit heart and soul sister, thank you for good morning and good night texts, listening to my monkey mind, sushi roll hugs, and for taking care of my sads while celebrating my not yet successes, and being the only person who keeps up with where I am when. You came into my world out of nowhere when I needed you most.

To the countless angels who opened your homes and your hearts and fed me on my journeys, I bow to you. Julie, Tim, and Semper Doble, thank you for always offering me a cozy bed, a hug, a home-cooked meal, a puppy wrestle, and a Labrador lean. And to Millie Doble, on the other side of the Rainbow Bridge, I hereby deem you Animal Companion of the Universe! Heather Veronica and Pam Flood, I can always turn on the voice recordings of your affirmations in my head and remember that at my core, I am beautiful and brilliant and wonderful and amazing. Eddie and Olivia, your raw vulnerability, your truths, your love, and your commitment to your own healing showed me the way as you held my hand. Tracey Mortensen, you were excited for me when I was scared. Lisa Sedlak, you held me when I couldn't hold myself. Laurie & Bryan Stave thank you for allowing me to leave my brokenness in the ashes of your fireplace as you wrapped me in the afghan love of your family cabin. Gary Stucchi, I wear the talisman you alchemically transformed from my wedding ring as my badge of empowerment, it never leaves me. Tairi Grace you break the boundaries, and move mountains all while walking barefoot and raising babies, and I'm honored that we share a first name. Natasha Bonilla and Elena Lund your sisterhood taught me to always love the men we have loved and, well, *here's to us*. Brenda David, your guest room is as cozy as your friendship, and I hope to return often to both. And to the countless others who served me soup, offered me gifts, gave me an overnight home, and held me as I cried, thank you.

To those who assisted directly with the writing and publishing process, I honor you. Alex Friend, thank you for giving me a hiding place to dig inside myself away from the world and write. Amanda Meyer, thank you for your vision and creating the image to match my story. Laura Muma, thank you for your diligence as my grammar and mechanics police. Jean Allie, my faerie godmother, your cozy backyard faerie cottage is the most enchanting home I ever inhabited. These pages are filled with the whisperings of the other worldly creatures who kept me company while I revised.

To my family, those of my blood and bones, I am blessed to be a part of the legacy and tradition that runs deep in our ancestry. Thank you all for instilling the values, wisdom, and blessings of my being.

And lastly, to Ted. Thank you for loving me enough to let me go.

The Gift Inside the Wound

Teri Leigh

www.ingramcontent.com/pod-product-compliance
Lightning Source LLC
Chambersburg PA
CBHW020932090426
42736CB00010B/1113